D1609510

Canal Street

New Orleans' Great Wide Way

Canal Street
New Orleans' Great Wide Way

PEGGY SCOTT LABORDE
AND
JOHN MAGILL

To Mary Ellen —
     All the best to you and
our great "Main Street"

     Peggy Suplestoe
     December, 2006

PELICAN PUBLISHING COMPANY
GRETNA 2006

*The word "Pelican" and the depiction of a pelican are trademarks
of Pelican Publishing Company, Inc., and are registered in the
U.S. Patent and Trademark Office.*

Library of Congress Cataloging-in-Publication Data

Laborde, Peggy Scott.
  Canal Street : New Orleans' great wide way / by Peggy Scott Laborde
and John Magill.
      p. cm.
  Includes bibliographical references and index.
  ISBN-13: 978-1-58980-337-4 (hardcover : alk. paper)
  1. Canal Street (New Orleans, La.)—Pictorial works. 2. Canal Street
(New Orleans, La.)—History. 3. New Orleans (La.)—Pictorial works.
4. New Orleans (La.)—Social life and customs. 5. New Orleans (La.)—
History. I. Magill, John T. II. Title.
  F379.N575C366 2006
  976.3'3500222—dc22

                                        2006010529

Printed in China
Published by Pelican Publishing Company, Inc.
1000 Burmaster Street, Gretna, Louisiana 70053

Contents

This postcard from the 1920s indicates the importance of Canal Street as a New Orleans version of New York's Broadway. Canal Street is actually wider than Broadway. (Courtesy of The Historic New Orleans Collection)

Acknowledgments

SPECIAL THANKS TO Priscilla Lawrence, executive director of The Historic New Orleans Collection, who suggested that I collaborate with John Magill. That suggestion will be fondly remembered as the best advice I have received in a long time. Also thanks to the Collection for sharing many of the photos that are in this book.

The foundation for this book was laid by two programs that I produced for New Orleans Public Broadcasting Service affiliate WYES-TV: "Canal Street: The Great Wide Way" and "Where New Orleans Shopped." For the former, thanks to John Lawrence, who helped curate an exhibit on Canal Street at The Historic New Orleans Collection in the 1980s. For the latter, I want to acknowledge Doris Ann Gorman, an accomplished researcher.

WYES-TV's Beth Utterback and Randall Feldman have long been supportive of local history documentaries. Without their interest in having such local programs as part of the station's schedule, the chances that this book would exist would be remote.

Helping to shape those Canal Street-related documentaries and thereby influencing this project are longtime colleagues David M. Jones and Stephen Tyler. Thanks also to Sidney Besthoff III, Sybil Morial, Dr. Raphael Cassimere, Jr., Yvonne LaFleur, and Adella Gautier. Their interviews, initially for the above-mentioned documentaries, proved invaluable.

Mark Larson, Hal Pluché, Larry Roussarie, Annette Campo, and Ashli Richard of WYES provided needed technical assistance. Adding encouragement were friends Patricia Brady and Dominic Massa.

Both John Magill and I want to thank Mary Lou Eichhorn of The Historic New Orleans Collection for her memory as well as computer expertise. Greg Lamboussy of the Louisiana State Museum, Dr. Charles Nolan of the Archdiocese of New Orleans Archive, Peter Finney, Jr. and Frank Methe III of the *Clarion Herald,* and Tulane University Library's Dr. Bill Meneray offered the utmost cooperation. And speaking of cooperation, the New Orleans Public Library's City Archivist Wayne Everard has stepped up and answered the question, "Do you have . . . ?" countless times. Also thanks to John Kemp, Robert Cangelosi, Sally Kittredge Reeves, and Jack Stewart for their always-helpful input.

Photographers Robert and Jan Brantley, Mitchel Osborne, Kerri

McCaffety, and Alex Demyan have contributed their talents to our book, making it all the more attractive.

Thanks also to Dr. Milburn Calhoun of Pelican Publishing Company for his faith in our project and to editors Nina Kooij and Jim Calhoun for their calm direction.

In the course of writing this book, Hurricane Katrina struck New Orleans. Providing in its wake a place not only for shelter and good cheer but also peace and quiet were Chris and Christine Normand of Marksville, Louisiana.

And now to members of my family: My mother, Gloria Walther Scott, who worked on Canal Street at D. H. Holmes for over twenty years, was truly my guide to the street's wonders and riches. Her mother, Antoinette Sickinger Walther, took me downtown as a tiny child and whetted my appetite. As with so many young visitors to the street, the dime stores such as Woolworth's were perfect places for making any money you had stretch far and wide. I can still smell the roasted nuts and remember buying Evening in Paris perfume and "kiddie" cosmetics. Much appreciation to my sister, Nancy Scott Degan, for her astute legal advice. Nancy, along with brother Kurt, also helped shape some of my fondest memories of Canal Street.

Finally, yet foremost, thanks to my husband, Errol Laborde, whose wisdom and continued support in so many ways makes my various journeys safe and pleasant ones. He also gives me the courage to venture into the sometimes-unexplored territory of New Orleans' recent past—a past of a city both of us never cease to love.

—PEGGY SCOTT LABORDE

Introduction

MY FONDEST MEMORIES of downtown Canal Street are after-school visits in the late 1960s to see my mother, Gloria Walther Scott, who worked for Revlon Cosmetics at D. H. Holmes Department Store. Dressed in a white parochial school blouse and a less than flattering broom-pleated, green plaid Cabrini High skirt, I would take the Esplanade Avenue bus through the French Quarter to downtown. This was a fairly uneventful bus ride except for the Esplanade and North Rampart Street stop where the students of all-male St. Aloyisius High got on. They conveyed their joy and relief at being out of school for the day with lots of chatter and kidding around.

Upon arrival at Mom's make-up counter, centrally located on the first floor right in the middle of D. H. Holmes across from the escalator, I would hand her my books and away I would go. What delicious freedom to mosey up and down Canal Street for a few hours!

Lerner's was a favorite stop. Clothes at the right price and the option of lay-away. Also a plus was the store's manager, the congenial Mr. Arnold. For shoes, I would visit Butler's, Burt's, or Baker's. With only an occasional visit

Lerner's was a popular chain of women's stores not only on Canal Street but across the United States. Alan J. Lerner, lyricist for such Broadway hits as My Fair Lady *and* Camelot, *was a member of the family. (Photo by C. F. Weber; courtesy of Bergeron Gallery)*

This aerial photograph of the river end of Canal Street in the 1950s shows the steamer President, *a popular excursion boat for daily tours and nightly concerts. One longtime house band was the Crawford-Ferguson Night Owls.*

to the Teen Fashions department at Maison Blanche and Kreeger's, I became a mostly Holmes customer since our family received the employee discount on all purchases.

A visit to Doubleday bookstore in the 600 block of Canal was a must. Only until later as an adult did I get to know the tall, thin, bespectacled bookstore manager George deVille, a shining light and mentor to many folks involved with the local literary scene. I would take my time combing through the books and records in the shop to overhear what seemed to be very witty and erudite conversation between deVille and his customers.

On Thursday evenings, most of the downtown stores would remain open until 8:30 P.M. My dad, brother, sister, and I would head downtown to pick up Mom after work. If we were a few minutes early, we'd venture to the foot of Canal at the Mississippi River to watch those lucky folks boarding the steamer *President* for the moonlight cruise. For many years the Crawford-Ferguson Night Owls played their bouncy jazz tunes as the vessel cruised up and down the river, affording a wonderful view of the almost 300-year-old city. I always thought how fortunate those passengers were. Very grown-up.

When I was in college, I worked part-time at D. H. Holmes as a "flyer," temporary help that would pinch-hit for a sick or vacationing employee. One day I would experience the boredom of the luggage department, the next, the hustle and bustle at the Russell Stover candy counter, especially during Easter season. My favorite assignment was the book department (with its good New Orleans history section), where I ended up spending much of what I earned.

During one Christmas season in the early 1970s, I worked in Holmes' men's department, known as Men's Furnishings, only a few feet away from my mother's Revlon counter. I must say I derived a lot of satisfaction helping wives match a shirt with the correct tie for their husbands. The thought that I had something to do with what went under the Christmas tree in many a home that season made me smile.

When it was time for Mom's coffee break, we'd go have a soft drink at the employee lounge one flight up in the rear of the department store. It was here that the mostly female employee work force would put their feet up for a few minutes and gossip. Also memorable were visits to the Holmes restaurant, with its uniformed waitresses and long marble counter surrounded by an L-shaped room of cafe tables. On the walls were quaint, dark oil paintings of swamp scenes and New Orleans views by George Castleden. Very sophisticated.

As someone who worked on Canal Street, I quickly learned what a village it was. There were the regular customers, the same ladies who would come downtown, perhaps sit for a few minutes in the ladies' lounge outside the public restrooms on the second floor of Holmes, and then move on to accomplish the tasks of the day. Familiar faces. A comfort comes from such familiarity.

The D. H. Holmes restaurant, as seen in the early 1920s, was replaced about a half-century later by the Potpourri Restaurant. (Courtesy of The Historic New Orleans Collection)

New Orleans artist and musician George Schmidt, who studied architecture at Tulane, has described Canal Street downtown as an "enormous room—particularly if you're coming from the French Quarter side. You're coming from a very tightly enclosed space, which is the European French Quarter, and then . . . bang! out into this huge space; not only do the dimensions change but there are new sounds, of traffic and people walking."

I agree with George. Downtown Canal Street is a big "room" with lots of doors. John Magill and I will explore some of them, both within and beyond the Central Business District. These are rooms filled with memories of a gathering place not only for shopping but for Christmas, Carnival, and sometimes even social upheaval. This is a place that contains much of our city's history and the hopes for its future.

—PEGGY SCOTT LABORDE

Introduction

MOST AMERICANS SAY "I'm going downtown" when they mean that they are going to take a trip to their city's business district. This term is most likely derived from references to going downtown in lower Manhattan in New York City, where once most of that city's shops and banks were located. In other parts of the English-speaking world, a person might say he or she is going into the city—perhaps a reference to the City, London's fabled financial district, or going to town, in reference to the shops and clubs of the fashionable West End of London. In some cities, people might talk about going to main street, and this is the case for people in New Orleans, where a trip downtown has long prompted the remark, "I'm going to Canal Street."

For over a century, Canal Street was not only where the biggest and finest stores in New Orleans were located but was also where there was the greatest variety. There were also the first-run theaters and the most popular restaurants for having a quick lunch—especially during a shopping trip. In New Orleans, if a downtown business was not on Canal Street, it would not have been much more than a block or two away. This is not meant to imply that New Orleans has a "one-street downtown"—most of the banks and office buildings have always been on nearby streets—but Canal Street was where everybody aspired to go and did so by saying, "I'm going to Canal Street."

Just about everybody dressed up in their best to go downtown in whichever city they lived, and to go downtown looking otherwise would have made anyone feel undressed. This was true in New Orleans. A gentleman would hardly ever go to Canal Street in casual attire, for suits, ties, and hats were *de rigueur*. For ladies, it was always dresses and black gloves in the winter—white gloves in the summer—and, of course, hats. Little wonder that until the end of the 1950s there was an abundance of hat stores on Canal Street—and some of these shops sold nothing but hats.

"Going to Canal Street" has been a rite of passage for youthful residents of New Orleans. For many school children, this has been a daily passage to and from school on public transportation, since Canal Street is a transfer point for many bus lines. This allows youngsters to pass through Canal Street or to just "hang out" there every afternoon. For every young person growing up in New Orleans, "going to Canal Street" was just part of growing up. A boy might buy his first good suit at a Canal Street department store, while a girl might purchase her first cosmetics on Canal Street—

Many city bus lines in New Orleans terminate on Canal Street, and as a result the street is often crowded with pedestrians transferring from one line to another. This was especially the case when most people still depended upon public transit. This is the intersection at Dauphine between Maison Blanche and D. H. Holmes about 1950. (Courtesy of The Historic New Orleans Collection)

probably at Woolworth's (always pronounced locally "Woolsworth's"), since Gus Mayer or Godchaux's cosmetics departments were more for grown-ups. In years past, perhaps a first summer or part-time Christmas job might have been at a Canal Street store.

While today shopping more often revolves around a shopping mall, in the past it usually revolved around certain department stores—be it D. H. Holmes, Maison Blanche, or Krauss. The experience sometimes went beyond buying. Not just for Ignatius Reilly in *A Confederacy of Dunces,* meeting under the clock at Holmes was legendary in New Orleans to the point that when the store was closed in the late 1980s, the clock was temporarily stolen by some nostalgic fans and put in "safekeeping."

The clock at Holmes did not have a long history in the scheme of things, going back only to the early twentieth century, but it had been around long enough that when it came down, few people could remember a day when the clock had not been hanging over the store's doorway.

But not everyone met under the Holmes clock. A few met by the elevators in the first-floor hallway of the Maison Blanche building. This tall Canal Street landmark has not always been just for shopping. It also has provided its own not always pleasant form of youthful rite of passage, since it housed the offices of many doctors, dentists, and optometrists who would have been reached via this bank of elevators. There were elevator operators still present there even after self-service elevators had come to most other stores.

Restaurants have long been a part of life on Canal Street. They were in the department stores, as well as on corners, to feed shoppers and office workers. In 1854 Thomas K. Wharton, superintendent of construction of the Custom House, wrote in his journal that he took a pleasant walk to have dinner and "delicious ices" at Vincent's confectionary at the corner of Canal and Carondelet streets, where ice cream, coffee, and chocolate were sold.

This statue of Ignatius Reilly, the curmudgeonly main character of the Pulitzer Prize-winning *A* Confederacy of Dunces, *waits for his mother like so many other locals under the* clock at Holmes. (Courtesy of Peggy Scott Laborde)

One of the popular eating spots on Canal Street for businessmen and shoppers looking for a good lunch was Meal-A-Minit at the corner of University Place. The dessert
specialty was a giant banana split. (Courtesy of Billy Gruber)

Meal-a-Minit Restaurant.

The purple-mirrored glass at Russell Stover's Candy Shop was at the corner of St. Charles Street. It was a Canal Street landmark for decades. (Courtesy of The Historic New Orleans Collection)

In the 1870s Canal Street was home to Moreau's Restaurant, between St. Charles and Carondelet streets. In its day it was considered the best restaurant in the city. By the twentieth century, Moreau's was gone, but lunch could be had at lunch counters and booths at restaurants such as Meal-a-Minit at the corner of University Place. There were also lunch counters at Katz & Besthoff, Woolworth's, and other dime stores, which would also become the sites of sit-ins during the civil rights movement of the early 1960s.

Virtually a trip back in time to the 1920s were fancier restaurants in the department stores, such as Holmes, where real paintings graced the walls until it was remodeled in the early 1970s to become the Potpourri. One of Holmes' more unique amenities was a big scale near the inside restaurant entrance. The scale's hand was large enough that nobody using it could misread the weight total.

A craving for sweets could be satisfied at the Holmes candy counter where, in season, customers could buy Louisiana strawberries dipped in chocolate. If D. H. Holmes was not chosen, there was also the candy counter at Maison Blanche, or the always-elegant Godchaux's, which sold gourmet Blum's chocolate of San Francisco. For years Russell Stover's candy shop with its purple glass stood out on Canal at St. Charles.

During the 1960s and 1970s—especially after Solari's on Royal Street closed—all but a few specialized grocers and supermarkets carried imported food. If one had a yen for delicacies such as Scottish marmalade, English tea, German jams, or the products of Fortnum and Mason of London, Fouchon of Paris, or S. S. Pierce of Boston, or anything else to tantalize, there was always the gourmet department at Holmes. This was tucked in the back of the Canal Street store, although it was later moved to the "Outback" annex along with the Holmes cafeteria on the other side of Iberville Street. At big holidays such as Thanksgiving and Christmas, Holmes could deliver a turkey with all the trimmings.

During the months after the end of World War II in 1945, the United States began welcoming a stream of new war brides, and as one of the nation's greatest ports, New Orleans was among the welcoming cities. One of those war brides was this writer's mother, Alison Magill, who as a 26-year-old arrived in the United States in October 1945 from Auckland, New Zealand. Aside from the American Panama Canal Zone and the muddy Mississippi water at the mouth of the river, my mother's first view of the United States was Canal Street. The low-rise Victorian and Edwardian buildings of Auckland's Queen Street might not have been too different from the buildings of the same era on Canal Street, although Canal was flatter, wider, much hotter, and "very busy."

My mother did what everyone was supposed to do on Canal Street. After just a few hours, she went shopping, and bought a black hat decorated with net at a hat shop she remembers as being on Canal near Royal. The next day, she left New Orleans to join my father, who was then stationed in Oklahoma. After a short return to New Orleans—when I happened to be born—and time spent living in Hawaii and California, they returned less than two decades later to New Orleans with me. This time it was to stay, and to go shopping on that street where a black hat was purchased so many years before. Even today, when my mother goes to "the city," she wears gloves.

—JOHN MAGILL

The corner of Canal and Exchange Place in 1953 showing Mack's, a popular restaurant and bar at the time, and the still-standing light standards installed in 1929-30. (Courtesy of The Historic New Orleans Collection)

Canal Street

New Orleans' Great Wide Way

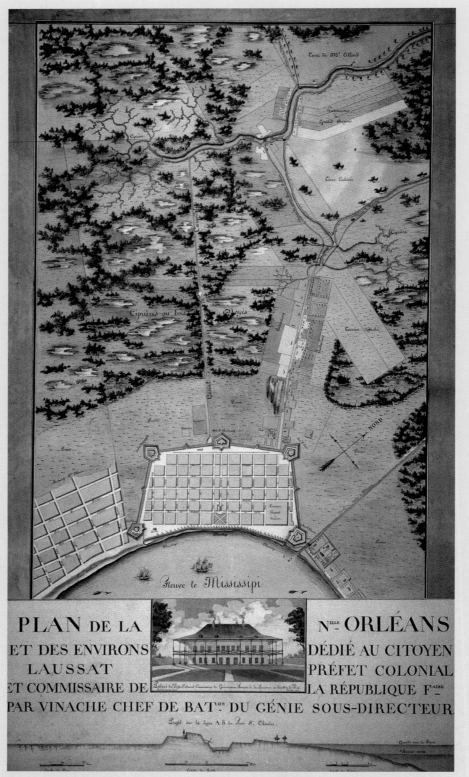

This 1803 map of New Orleans by French surveyor Joseph Antoine Vinache shows the green commons between the French Quarter and today's Common Street. A canal was planned on the Commons, but it was not built and Canal Street evolved instead. (Courtesy of The Historic New Orleans Collection)

CHAPTER ONE
The Early Days

CANAL STREET WAS born—but not in name—in 1807, and in a sense was an outgrowth of the 1803 Louisiana Purchase. A wide space called the Commune de la Ville, or the City Commons, surrounded the French Quarter and also separated the Quarter from Faubourg St. Mary, the city's oldest suburb, which was established in 1788 and today is the city's Central Business District. The Commons was European Crown land where there had been an earth and timber palisade and five forts to protect the city.

The five forts were Fort St. Charles, near the Mississippi River and modern Esplanade Avenue, Fort St. John, near Esplanade and North Rampart Street, Fort St. Ferdinand, at Congo Square in front of the modern Morris F. X. Jeff Auditorium, Fort Bourgoyne, near the intersection of Canal Street and North Rampart Street, and Fort St. Louis, near Canal and Tchoupitoulas streets.

With the Louisiana Purchase of 1803, the Crown property went to the United States government. In 1806 the land was given to French noble-man the Marquis de la Fayette, of American Revolutionary War fame. But when New Orleans objected, the United States ceded the land to the city with the stipulation that a navigation canal be constructed along part of the land to connect the Mississippi River and Lake Pontchartrain.

A plan was drawn up by city surveyor Jacques Tanesse, dated April 15, 1809, and titled rather lengthily

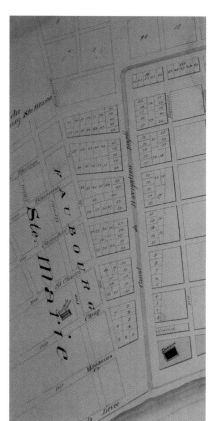

Jacques Tanesse in 1810 subdivided the City Commons, shown here on an 1812 map of New Orleans. The canal was planned where Canal Street eventually would be established. (Courtesy of The Historic New Orleans Collection)

MARK TWAIN, FROM *LIFE ON THE MISSISSIPPI* (1883)

From Chapter 41, "The Metropolis of the South," on visiting New Orleans in the late 1850s:

"Canal Street was finer, and more attractive and stirring than formerly, with its drifting crowds of people, its several processions of hurrying street-cars and—toward evening—its broad second-story verandas crowded with gentlemen and ladies clothed according to the latest mode."

21

This view of the Canal Street shopping district on a summer day in 1952 by Charles L. Franck Photographers clearly shows the great expanse of the proposed canal route. (Courtesy of The Historic New Orleans Collection)

> Plan drawn up in execution of the decree of the City Council of New Orleans approved by the mayor the 15 June 1807, relative to the six hundred yards of its Commons, starting from its fortifications on all sides, on which a right of ownership has been recognized to the said city by the United States.

Soon after, all of the fortifications except Fort St. Charles were removed, and in 1810 Tanesse began subdividing the Commons that included Esplanade Avenue and North Rampart Street.

On the upriver side of the Commons Tanesse set aside space for a fifty-foot-wide waterway flanked by two sixty-foot-wide roadways. This was a total width of 170 feet, only one foot less than the width of modern Canal Street. The canal to the lake was not designed as a straight line, but rather extended out from the river levee to what is now Basin Street.

At that point it would turn at a right angle to join the basin of the Carondelet Canal, later called the Old Basin Canal, which had been built in the 1790s. This canal ran along what is now Lafitte Street. It intersected with the tip of Bayou St. John, which ultimately led to Lake Pontchartrain. The Carondelet Canal was not designed to actually intersect with the waters of the Mississippi since that would have produced a serious river flooding problem.

The Orleans Navigation Company was established to finance and construct what was deemed a nationally important transportation route reflecting the monumental importance of the Mississippi River at the time. Lake Pontchartrain and Bayou St. John had formed a major route to the city from the Gulf of Mexico, and a navigation canal between the river and the lake had long been a dream. This dream would have to wait, since the proposed navigation canal on Tanesse's plan was not carried out. There were some canals connecting the river and the lakes such as the

Lake Borgne Canal of the 1840s in St. Bernard Parish. But a large-scale navigation canal did not materialize until 1923 when the Inner Harbor Navigation Canal, better known as the Industrial Canal, was dedicated.

At first Canal Street grew slowly on its path to becoming the heart of commercial New Orleans. In its earliest years after the Commons was subdivided, the street was virtually in the country, with buildings along its route widely scattered except for a concentration near the river at Tchoupitoulas and Levee (Decatur) streets—which was then the Mississippi riverfront.

The character of the modern business portion of Canal Street—between the river and Claiborne Avenue—has gone through several distinct periods of change, change representing not only the growing wealth and importance of the street, but nearly two centuries of architectural fashion.

A late-1850s bird's-eye view of Canal Street by Jay Dearborn Edwards from the top of the United States Custom House. The median was still undeveloped, although by the end of the decade funds from the estate of Judah Touro would pay for the street's beautification. (Courtesy of The Historic New Orleans Collection)

By the 1840s and 1850s, Canal Street was lined with rows of low-rise three- and four-story buildings. By the 1870s, buildings had more ornamentation, such as elaborate rooflines with spires and cupolas. In the late 1880s, early "skyscrapers" such as the Morris, long known as the Cigali Building, rose to seven stories. After that, progressively taller buildings such as the 1902 Imperial Building (Godchaux's Clothing Store until the 1980s) and the 1909 Maison Blanche structure would further raise the street's skyline. With a few exceptions, Canal Street's panorama would remain relatively unaltered until the decades after the 1960s when real skyscrapers made their appearance at the river end of the street.

Today, several buildings survive from the 1820s and 1830s, and these give us an impression of what the street would have once looked like. The oldest building on the street stretches between Decatur Street and Dorsiere Place. Dating from 1821, it is typical of many buildings at the time, since it served both commercial and residential purposes, although it was remodeled to its present look in 1899 and is now the home of a Wendy's fast-food restaurant. At the corner of Royal Street are three matching stone buildings built in 1825 by Germain Musson, grandfather of French Impressionist painter Edgar Degas. These are among the earliest large commercial structures on the street.

Directly across Canal Street from the Musson Buildings at the corner of St. Charles Street is one of the remaining structures of what was built as a row of three buildings in 1833. It is typical of small commercial buildings built on Canal Street at the time. For many years it has housed part of Rubenstein Brothers clothing store. This fine store is a complex of fine old commercial buildings whose facades above the ground floors have barely changed since the late nineteenth century.

Beyond Royal Street, Canal became progressively more residential

Marie Adrien Persac's 1873 drawing of Canal Street between Decatur and Chartres shows the oldest building on the street at the far right prior to its 1899 restoration. The area at the left is now occupied by the Marriott Hotel. (Courtesy of The Historic New Orleans Collection)

The oldest still-standing building on Canal Street, seen here during World War I, is at the corner of Decatur. The building, which dates from the 1820s, was remodeled in 1899 and now houses a Wendy's Restaurant. (Courtesy of The Historic New Orleans Collection)

This 1873 Marie Adrien Persac's drawing of Canal Street between Chartres and Royal, with Exchange Place between, shows what is today one of the least-changed blocks on the street. The still-standing buildings owned by Edgar Degas' relatives, the Musson family, are visible at the left at Royal Street. (Courtesy of The Historic New Orleans Collection)

One of the few buildings from the 1840s that still stands was built for Newton Mercer, a physician, as his residence. Today it is the home of the Boston Club. (Courtesy of The Historic New Orleans Collection)

about the 1830s as it witnessed the construction of some of the city's finer townhouses. In the heart of Canal Street is one of its finest mid-nineteenth century townhouses still standing. It is now the home of the Boston Club, a private men's club that has been there since 1884. The club took its name from a card game. The house and side garden remain hardly changed from when they were built in the 1840s for Dr. Newton Mercer.

At one time the block between University Place and South Rampart Street was lined with opulent townhouses. The most notable mansion and garden on the block were built in 1856 for F. W. Tilton at the corner of University Place. The grand house became the Shakespeare Literary and Theatrical Club by 1873; by 1900, however, the house was no longer standing.

Beginning in the 1840s, additional grandly proportioned townhouses were appearing on Canal Street beyond Rampart Street alongside more modest rows of houses. By the early twentieth century, many of these houses had become tenements, although the buildings still remained recognizable. Today, only a handful of the buildings are standing. and they have become so neglected under the guise of commercial alterations and signage that they are hardly recognizable.

Separating the two roadways of Canal Street and the quaintness of the French Quarter and dynamism of the business district is the median, which is locally called the "neutral ground." Indeed, the term has come to define every median in the area. Initially the term meant a common ground, a dividing line between the French-speaking Creole natives and the newly arrived Americans. By the mid-nineteenth century, Orleanians of all classes and backgrounds gathered on Canal Street to shop, do business, and transfer from one streetcar line to another—thus, this was the "neutral ground" for all New Orleanians.

Outside the business district, as the street developed, street names were given a north and south designation. But downtown Canal Street became the great gathering place and center of activity in New Orleans. With all manner of events occurring on the thoroughfare, it became the equivalent of Times Square in New York or Piccadilly Circus in London.

As large stores proliferated along Canal Street in the 1850s and streetcar lines terminated there, people gravitated more and more to its confines. Because of its great width, it could accommodate larger crowds than most other main streets. Canal Street has been called America's widest main street, and while some towns, including Augusta, Georgia, have disputed this, few big cities have a main street that is as wide as some entire city blocks.

The largest building on early Canal Street was Charity Hospital, which was built in 1815 between Baronne Street and University Place. In 1832 the hospital moved to new quarters on Common, now Tulane Avenue. The state capitol was moved into the former hospital building. In 1815 the building was still considered "in the country," but by the 1830s the fast-growing city was quickly expanding around it.

In 1834 traveler Joseph Holt Ingraham wrote of the statehouse:

> Its snow-white front, though plain, is very imposing; and the whole structure with its handsome, detached wings, and large green [lawn], thickly covered with shrubbery in front, luxuriant with orange and lemon trees, presents decidedly, one of the finest views to be met with in the city.

Ingraham went on to describe the rest of the Canal Street "with its triple row of young sycamores, extending through out the whole length," as

> one of the most spacious, and destined at no distant period to be one of the first and handsomest streets of the city. Every building in the street is of modern construction, and some blocks of its brick edifices will vie in tasteful elegance with the boasted granite piles of Boston.

The street, though wide, was not long, and Ingraham wrote that "this street, which less than a mile from the river terminates in the swampy commons, every where surrounding New Orleans, except the river side." Thus, he described Canal Street as disappearing into the swamps somewhere around Claiborne Avenue. Ultimately, the street would extend almost 3½ miles, with its terminus, quite appropriately, in front of a grouping of cemeteries.

The state legislature moved from New Orleans to Donaldsonville, and then to Baton Rouge in the late 1840s, and the elegant capitol Ingraham described—then only about thirty-five years old and surrounded by the fast growing city—was sold and demolished. The block on which it stood was quickly covered with a mixture of residences and commercial establishments, but within a short time, commerce would

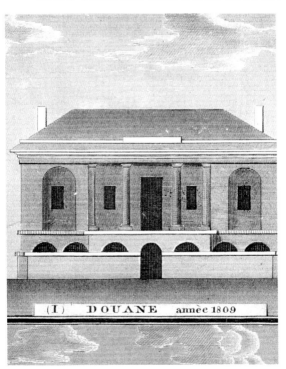

The Custom House as it appeared in the early 1800s. This is one of three Custom House buildings, each larger than its predecessor, that has occupied the site. (Courtesy of The Historic New Orleans Collection)

come to absorb the entire block. As with the rest of Canal Street's commercial heart, once business took hold the former residential character never returned.

Established in 1805, Christ Episcopal Church is the oldest Protestant congregation in Louisiana, and for about eighty years the church called Canal Street home. The congregation worshiped in several locations, including the Cabildo. In 1816, it moved into an octagonal brick building designed by Henry S. Latrobe, son of the famous English-born architect of the first United States capitol, Benjamin Latrobe, on the river side of Bourbon Street.

By the 1830s the congregation had outgrown its small church, and in 1837 a new one was built on the same site. Designed by James Dakin and James Gallier, Sr. with a row of six Ionic columns and no steeple, it resembled nothing more than a Greek temple. It survived less than ten years, since in 1846 a new Christ Church was built on the lakeside corner of

View of Canal Street looking toward Lake Pontchartrain from Bourbon in the late 1850s, by Jay Dearborn Edwards. The steeple of Christ Episcopal Church is at the right. (Courtesy of The Historic New Orleans Collection)

Canal Steet in 1866. (Photo by Theodore Lilienthal; courtesy of the Louisiana State Museum)

Dauphine Street. It was designed by Thomas K. Wharton and built by James Gallier, Sr. in the Gothic style, which was regarded as more fitting for an Episcopal house of worship. For nearly four decades Christ Church dominated the skyline of Canal Street as the street's tallest structure.

In 1887 the church building—just about forty years old—was demolished after the congregation moved to its current home on St. Charles Avenue at Sixth Street. Its replacement was the ornate Mercier Building, which

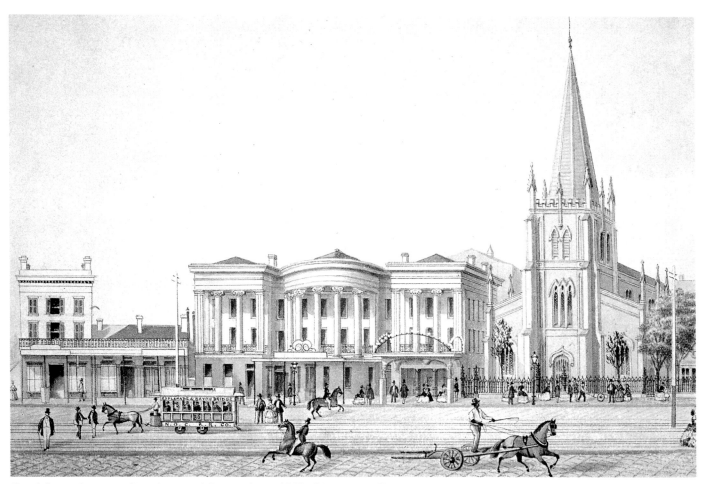

Canal Street between Dauphine and Burgundy in 1873. Shown are Christ Episcopal Church and Union Terrace, to the left of the church. Later, Maison Blanche Department Store occupied most of the block. Today, the Ritz-Carlton Hotel and the Audubon Building fill the block. This is one of twenty detailed block elevations of Canal Street by Marie Adrien Persac. (Courtesy of The Historic New Orleans Collection)

During the late nineteenth century, many grandiose buildings appeared on Canal Street. The Crescent Brewery, on the downtown corner of North Claiborne and Canal Street, became a candy factory during Prohibition.

became the first home of Maison Blanche Department Store in 1897. Commerce had truly come to dominate this portion of Canal Street.

The distinctive golden beehive corner dome of this building would dominate the corner of Canal and Dauphine for only about thirty years—there was no preservation movement then. Around 1908 it was torn down for a new Maison Blanche "skyscraper" store and office building that still stands on the site as the Ritz-Carlton Hotel.

CHAPTER TWO

Shopping

As NEW ORLEANS grew to become one of the largest cities in the United States—the fourth largest, with a population of 102,000 in 1840—and one of the wealthiest, it also became one of the most important retail and wholesale centers on the continent. Despite its isolated location, the city actually evolved into a fairly fashion-conscious community as early as the late eighteenth century.

In 1803 this was noted by Pierre Clément Laussat, the French colonial prefect assigned by Napoleon the task of officially transferring Louisiana from France to the United States after the Louisiana Purchase. He wrote of how closely women in New Orleans followed current Paris modes and the expense this entailed. He found that living in New Orleans was rather expensive and actually asked for a pay raise from his superiors in Paris.

By the 1830s and 1840s, the center of high-class retail trade in New Orleans was located mostly along Chartres and Royal streets in the French Quarter. A visiting German nobleman extolled the quality of merchandise found there, and compared it with what could be found in London—then the world's shopping mecca—or Paris. This testifies to the wealth, taste, and drawing power of the New Orleans market when it was the shopping destination for the entire southern United States. The stores were for the most part small and highly specialized. In her memoirs, Eliza Ripley recalled that in the early 1840s most shops had a single door and a small window. Once inside, the shopper would usually find only certain fabrics, notions, or bonnets dispensed at a single counter with storage shelves behind.

By the 1840s, retail trade across Europe and America was changing and expanding dramatically, and Canal Street found itself in the midst of this rapid change. It soon became one of the most fashionable selling streets in the nation.

While small specialized shops—especially the more expensive variety—were the norm in early nineteenth century America, larger dry goods stores were beginning to make their appearance in New York and Philadelphia. These were not department stores in today's sense, but dealers primarily in fabric goods, notions, and accessories. Unlike stores on Royal or Chartres streets, these had expanded floor space, eye-catching displays of merchandise, and an abundance of light, either from skylights or artificial illumination. Gas began to be used in America around 1810,

LINDY BOGGS REMEMBERS

Lindy Boggs, former ambassador to the Holy See in the Vatican and member of the United States Congress, grew up in New Roads, Louisiana, but often came to New Orleans with family and friends. Here is her earliest memory of Canal Street as a four-year-old during the 1920s:

"My father died when I was 2½ years old," recalls Lindy Boggs, "and my mother had many suitors. One of them took me to Canal Street. We passed by the windows at Gus Mayer when it used to be next to D. H. Holmes, and I stopped in front of a beautifully dressed little girl mannequin in the window and decided that I wanted her. Uncle Ham, as I called him, said, 'That's not a doll, dear. It's a mannequin.' I sat down on the ground and wouldn't budge. He went in to get a salesperson to try to explain the difference but I just wouldn't budge. I went home with my 'doll' and had her until I was fourteen."

"LOOK AT ALMOST ANY CORNER . . ."

"Look at almost any corner, and what do you see?" the jingle went, "a big purple sign that says friendly "K&B." From Canal Street came a chain of stores, a camera shop, and even a brand of ice cream. When the color purple comes up in conversation in New Orleans, don't be surprised to hear *K&B purple* as a wistful reference point.

KB was shorthand for a locally owned drugstore chain that had such a loyal following that its passing is mourned by many locals to this day. To be more precise, "K&B" referred to the initials of Gustave Katz and Sydney J. Besthoff, two pharmacists who decided to go into business together in 1905. Their first apothecary was located downtown at 732 Canal Street. Almost a century later, the business would comprise 186 stores in six states when it was sold to the Florida-based Rite-Aid drugstore chain.

Mr. Katz remained an active

The first of what grew to over 180 Katz & Besthoff drugstores was located on Canal Street. The store opened in 1905. (Courtesy of Sidney Besthoff III)

but was not introduced in New Orleans until ten years later. By the 1880s the city had become electrified. There were also large, decorated show windows, which at first were multiple panes of glass, since plate glass was not used until the 1860s.

As elevators were perfected in the 1850s, multi-floor stores became more common. Such new amenities made shopping not only easier and more pleasant, but more luxurious, thus turning buying into more of an experience. As the nineteenth century progressed, and shops become more elegant, some big stores, including D. H. Holmes, became something almost akin to mercantile cathedrals even better able to separate customers from their money.

Royal and Chartres streets, where most buildings had narrow frontages and limited floor space, could not accommodate the modern dry goods establishments with their expanse of floors and show windows; but Canal Street, just a short distance away, could offer the necessary space for such expansion. In the early 1840s, there were already a few shops on Canal Street among the townhouses and other commercial places, but the thoroughfare did not have the reputation of a fashionable shopping center. By the late 1840s this began to change.

D. H. Holmes Department Store, named after founder Daniel Henry Holmes, was the first real dry goods emporium on Canal Street. Born in Ohio, Holmes came to New Orleans and opened his first store on Magazine Street in 1842. He then moved to more fashionable quarters on Chartres Street, but the popular merchant soon outgrew this space and in 1849 took the leap to a spacious new building on Canal Street between Bourbon and Dauphine.

By 1906 when this photograph was taken by John Teunisson, D. H. Holmes had evolved into a full-scale department store and was arranged in a cruciform floor plan that would hardly change. The store closed in 1989. (Courtesy of the New Orleans Public Library)

D. H. Holmes was known for its stylish windows throughout the store's history. This photograph was taken in 1916. (Courtesy of The Historic New Orleans Collection)

This was the early nucleus of a much-expanded store that would remain in business on the same site until the late 1980s. Holmes' long, narrow building extended halfway through the block and was illuminated by gas. The structure had two large show windows for displays on either side of the front door. To entice browsers—and hopefully buyers—Holmes installed an oversized, ornately framed French mirror at the back of the store where young ladies were encouraged to meet—a pastime not so different from young people's "hanging out" in today's shopping malls.

Like many dry goods stores of the day, D. H. Holmes absorbed adjoining buildings so that by 1870 there were entrances facing Bourbon, Dauphine, and Customhouse (now Iberville) streets, along with the main doors on Canal Street. Until its closing day, D. H. Holmes' main entrance was on Canal Street. Decorated in the Tudor Gothic style, D. H. Holmes in the nineteenth century was undoubtedly the most elegant store in the city. Through the 1880s it was primarily a ladies store selling a huge array of fabrics, notions, and accessories.

There was a large staff of dressmakers and seamstresses, since few off the rack clothes were available in any of the better establishments such as Holmes. Located near the center of the store was the silk room, and under its magnificent two-story vaulted Gothic ceiling customers made a point of wearing their best outfits to see and be seen.

Such an environment was designed to give the shoppers an elevated feeling that would encourage them to more willingly dispense with their cash. This attitude toward dressiness continued to exist on Canal Street—and on virtually every big-city main street—well into the mid-twentieth century, when ladies wore gloves (white in summer, please)

partner until his death in 1940; his family sold their interest to the Besthoff family. So where did the purple come from? According to company president Sidney J. Besthoff III, grandson of one of the founders:

The purple started because in those days everything was wrapped with brown paper and tied with brown string. My grandmother bought a lot of purple paper that somebody had rejected and started wrapping packages with it and all of sudden they realized when you saw people on Canal Street, you could tell immediately where they were shopping by looking at the color of the paper. At one time the *Times-Picayune* was the largest user of purple ink in America for our ads.

Canal Street was ultimately home to three K&B drugstores,

Confectionary shops and soda counters were common along Canal Street. Some were found in drugstores, while others were more specialized and quite elegant such as the well-known Fuerst and Kramer, shown here about 1910, which was in the same block as D. H. Holmes. When the store closed, Katz & Besthoff drugstores purchased this establishment's formula for nectar flavoring and achieved its own following for its nectar soda. (Courtesy of The Historic New Orleans Collection)

the second one at the corner of Canal and Dauphine streets and the third next to Sacred Heart of Jesus Roman Catholic Church in the Mid-City neighborhood. A soda fountain quickly became a store fixture, with nectar soda a favorite menu item.

Besthoff recalls:

> Nectar sodas were developed by a confectionary firm on Canal Street called Fuerst and Kramer, which operated on Canal. When they went out of business in the 1910s we bought the formula from them. My wife's forebears are from one of the families that ran Fuerst and Kramer, so you might say we got together seventy-five years later. In New Orleans everything runs together.

In addition to nectar sodas and its own brand of ice cream, K&B provided a soda fountain lunch, a highlight of many a shopper's day. For Besthoff, "the chicken salad, lettuce and tomato on toasted bread—it could not have been better!"

Pencils, liquor, even playing

At one time there were three Katz & Besthoff drugstores on Canal Street. The soda fountain at the K&B at the corner of Canal and Dauphine streets was a popular spot for both breakfast and lunch. (Courtesy of Sidney Besthoff III)

When built during the 1850s, the Touro Buildings on Canal Street between Royal and Bourbon housed some of the most fashionable shops in New Orleans. The buildings marked the first major use of cast iron on Canal Street and helped popularize it along the street. This is how the buildings appeared about 1870. (Courtesy of The Historic New Orleans Collection)

and hats, and men wore suits and hats. This was the norm for shopping, rather than a quaint exception. As D. H. Holmes continued to acquire buildings and add floors to its complex, by the twentieth century new departments—including furniture and household goods—helped create a full-fledged department store in the modern sense.

The next great step in Canal Street's development as New Orleans' and the South's greatest shopping street was construction of the Touro Buildings between Royal and Bourbon streets. When Christ Church moved from its old Bourbon Street corner, the building was traded to Jewish businessman and philanthropist Judah Touro, who assisted in the financing of the new Christ Church. He then converted the former church into the synagogue of the Dispersed of Judah—Touro Synagogue.

The building served in this capacity for only a few years. Then, during the 1850s, along with the rest of the buildings between Royal and Bourbon streets, it was replaced by a row of twelve buildings with a common facade housing fashionable shops and offices called the Touro Buildings, or the Touro Block. This was an upscale development that became one of the finest structures along nineteenth century Canal Street, in spirit not unlike modern mixed-use complexes such as Canal Place.

With its array of elegant dry goods, notions, music, and jewelry stores, the Touro Block became one of the most fashionable and desirable rows of modern shops in the nation. It was highlighted by large, gas-lit show windows that stretched the full 300-foot length of the block and, in the fashion of the day, were filled from top to bottom with the latest merchandise.

The chief retail tenants of the Touro Buildings were dry goods dealers and notions and accessory shops catering to female customers. Although there were a few men's shops such as Moody's, at the corner of Royal Street, and Walshe's, near St. Charles Street, the main shopping area of Canal Street was devoted mostly to women's fashion.

In the early 1870s, when most women still made their own clothes, nine of the ten New Orleans sewing machine dealers were located on Canal Street. There were other shopping streets in New Orleans—including Chartres, Royal, Magazine, and Dryades streets—but Canal Street was the city's showplace. Here were the best and most up-to-date dry

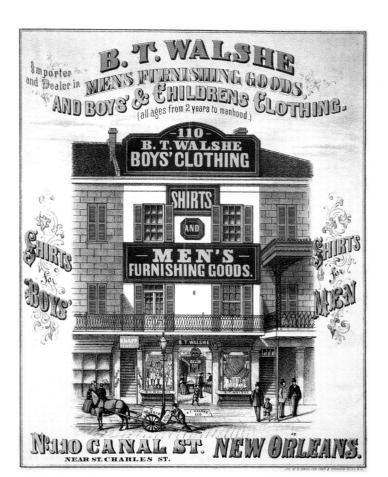

While Canal Street in the late nineteenth century was a venue for lady shoppers, there were several men's shirt shops and haberdasheries. One was B. T. Walshe's, seen here about 1870 where part of Rubenstein Brothers now stands near St. Charles. (Courtesy of The Historic New Orleans Collection)

Katz & Besthoff was once the most popular chain of drugstores in New Orleans and could be found at several locations on Canal Street. Shown here is one of its displays photographed by Charles L. Franck Photographers in 1951. (Courtesy of The Historic New Orleans Collection)

cards bore the K&B logo and familiar purple. "My grandmother loved playing cards," recalls Besthoff. In many a local kitchen utility drawer one could likely spot purple pencils or a pack of purple cards. The pencil may now be almost stubble, the deck creased and probably missing a card or two. But we wouldn't trade this stuff for anything, since it reminds us of the days we could look on almost any corner and find comfort in the color purple.

goods dealers, the best jewelers and silver sellers, the best carpet dealers, the best dressmakers and hatmakers.

The most fashionable dressmaker in New Orleans was French-born Madame Olympe, referred to by some gentlemen of New Orleans as "that old imp," because of her high prices. She began business on Chartres Street in the 1850s, but by the 1870s had relocated to a former townhouse on Canal Street. She remained on the street until her demise in the 1880s. New Orleans—and especially Canal Street—was the undisputed center of fashion in the nineteenth century South, and it is little wonder that Scarlett O'Hara went clothes shopping on her New Orleans honeymoon with Rhett Butler in *Gone with the Wind*.

Advertising was a growing business by the mid-nineteenth century, and on Canal Street where Chartres and Camp streets meet there was an elaborate form of advertising. The Belknap Fountain was erected in 1871 by Jackson Ogden Belknap, a Mobile, Alabama, foundry owner. An elaborate twenty-two-foot-tall cast-iron pavilion typical of the Gilded Age, the fountain contained a water-powered display of boats, cupids, and

CONVERSATION WITH A FAN

Milliner and dress shop owner Yvonne LaFleur, whose store has been a fixture in the Riverbend section of New Orleans for over thirty years, got her start in the retail business as a teenager on Canal Street. Her memories of the street go back to her childhood:

Q: Yvonne, what are your earliest memories of retail and shopping in New Orleans?

A: Well, I came to New Orleans when I was four years old on a train from San Francisco. My mom and I were relocating to stay with some of her sisters, who lived in an old house on Camp Street. So we got off at the L&N Train Station on Canal Street and took the street-car to 828 Canal Street, Godchaux's, where my aunt worked on the seventh floor. She did the

Millinery and dress shop owner Yvonne Owens LaFleur worked at many stores along Canal Street. (Photo courtesy of Yvonne LaFleur)

The Belknap Fountain was an elaborate, cast-iron advertising kiosk on Canal Street where Camp and Chartres meet. Erected in the early 1870s, it was moved to City Park during the 1890s. (Courtesy of The Historic New Orleans Collection)

swans that was illuminated by gas after dark. While it contained a drinking fountain, the structure consisted of advertising space where removable glass panels were used for paid advertisements.

With the appearance of electric streetcars beginning in 1893, the structure was used as a shelter for car starters, but at the same time the fountain had become a traffic obstacle. Ownership of the fountain fell to the city, and having outlived its usefulness, it was moved to the North Alexander Street entrance of City Park near the Pizatti Gate. By 1913 the rusting structure had been converted to an aviary. Today, it is said that it is still somewhere—perhaps on an island—within the vast expanse of the park.

One of the more innovative new stores to open on late nineteenth century Canal Street was Maison Blanche, also known as "MB." An outgrowth of an earlier dry goods store, Maison Blanche opened in 1897 in the elegant five-story Mercier Building at the corner of Dauphine—once the site of Christ Church. It was less than a block from its big dry goods competitor, D. H. Holmes. Maison Blanche opened with great fanfare and excitement, and was regarded in media coverage as the first real New York-style department store in New Orleans. It was not only a full-line department store but had about 130 feet of large, plate glass show windows along Canal Street. The windows were embellished throughout with mirrors and illuminated by rows of electric light bulbs that not only brilliantly lighted the window display but blazed light into the street as well.

New stores continued to join earlier pioneers on Canal Street, but virtually all of them came and went with time. One of the largest and best was J. Levois and Jamison, which was housed in a fine five-story building

As did many New Orleans teenage girls, Yvonne Owens LaFleur, on the right, modeled in fashion shows sponsored by Gus Mayer, D. H. Holmes, and other Canal Street clothing stores.

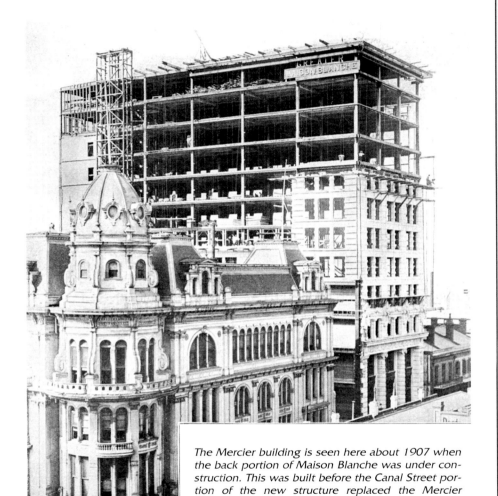

The Mercier building is seen here about 1907 when the back portion of Maison Blanche was under construction. This was built before the Canal Street portion of the new structure replaced the Mercier Building, allowing Maison Blanche to remain open throughout the building process. (Courtesy of The Historic New Orleans Collection)

One of the finest fashion stores in New Orleans for well over a century was Leon Godchaux's, which occupied this building between Carondelet and Baronne from the mid-1920s until its closure in the late 1980s. The current year was displayed over the entrance until the end.

billing. Immediately I was introduced to all the executives, and it was a wonderful experience.

Q: And when are we talking about?

A: This is '51. And so that was my

first experience. [I remember] the smell of walking through Godchaux's. They had the Antoine Hair Salon so the whole store had this wonderful "perfumey" smell, and was just beautiful. The store was just gorgeous. There was marble, the windows were beautiful, and I fell in love with retail instantly when I saw this store. Across the street my aunt worked for D. H. Holmes in the sportswear department as a saleslady for thirty-five years, and another aunt worked at Maison Blanche, running the elevator, so I got a full experience of New Orleans retail my very first day in New Orleans.

Q: How did you get to Canal Street?

A: The bus. The bus was seven cents. It was wonderful, In fact, as I got a little bit older, past ten, for seventy-five cents three days a week my mother had me completely out of her hair. I would take seven cents for the bus from the Ninth Ward, go all the way to Canal Street, walk over to Charity Hospital where I did volunteer work, fold gauze bandages, and buy a nickel coke and a nickel candy bar. And then walk over to visit my aunts in the department stores. And my aunt would definitely put me to good use at D. H. Holmes. She'd make me clean her fitting rooms and hang up all her clothes, because she was a very good salesperson. What a wonderful "growing up."

Q: You worked at many of the stores on Canal Street. Tell me about the character of some of these places.

A: Well, I worked from one end of

located between St. Charles and Carondelet streets during the 1860s and 1870s. Upon the store's demise, the building became a dime museum, which featured unusual exhibits, freak shows, and circus and theater performances designed for primarily working-class audiences. Next door to Levois and Jamison's building was H. B. Stevens Men's Store. Built in the early 1880s, Stevens ranked among the city's finest haberdashers. In the 1970s it merged with its elegant Baronne Street competitor Porter's to become Porter-Stevens.

The downtown—or French Quarter—side of Canal Street was where the department and variety stores concentrated. Aside from Holmes and Maison Blanche, there was the Krauss Company, at the corner of Basin Street. Krauss began in 1903 in a two-story building extending along the entire block. With a series of expansions beginning in 1912, Krauss created a five-story building covering an entire city block, and in the 1950s it leaped across Iberville as part of its continued expansion.

Between 1897 and 1917, the famed red-light district of Storyville was just outside the back door of Krauss, and the store proved to be a popular shopping spot for the ladies of the district. Although it was a block from the fringes of the main shopping district, Krauss thrived and grew until the late 1990s when it joined the increasing numbers of Canal Street closures. Like many old-fashioned stores in New Orleans, Krauss catered to its loyal local customers by maintaining a full sewing department long after most other department stores—many of which had been born primarily as fabric and dry goods stores—had abandoned that line of merchandising.

Krauss was also one of the city's few purveyors of women's hats in the years after hats had gone out of fashion. Krauss was popular with black shoppers,

Krauss Department Store lighted up for its fiftieth anniversary in 1953. This popular department store attracted customers from the notorious Storyville red-light district located across the street from the store's rear entrance. Krauss became famous for its fabric and hat departments. (Courtesy of Hugo Kahn)

This Krauss "dollar" was an early version of a gift certificate. (Courtesy of Hugo Kahn)

Marks Isaacs Department Store, seen here in 1946, operated on this site between Royal and Bourbon from the early twentieth century until it closed in the 1960s. The Hotel Astor Crown Plaza occupies the old building, which has a restored 1920s facade. (Courtesy of The Historic New Orleans Collection)

and for many black women, hats continue to be considered proper church attire.

Marks Isaacs Department Store was located between Royal and Bourbon streets in the center of the old Touro Block. One of the city's smaller department stores, it had its dry goods roots on Dryades Street in the late nineteenth century. The store moved to Canal Street in 1904, and in 1919 the store was rebuilt and a new facade was added. Marks Isaacs sold clothing and small household goods until it ceased business during the late 1960s. It was one of the first Canal Street department stores to go out of business.

In retailing, expansion is regarded one of the keys to success, and department stores such as Holmes, Maison Blanche, and Krauss steadily expanded throughout their histories on Canal Street. In the case of Holmes, the store expanded by absorbing neighboring sites and constructing new buildings. Holmes obtained virtual control of its entire block, except for Canal Street, where other retailers held onto their important main street locations. By the 1890s, Holmes' Canal Street front was able to at least double, and in 1912 a new facade of white-glazed terra cotta was built, along with an arcade of show windows and heavy wooden doors.

In 1965 an airy new facade was added, with rows of show windows extending back from the street to the entrance. The old-fashioned heavy doors were eliminated and replaced by a fully open entrance where a burst of air conditioning welcomed customers during the summer. It resembled the open entries found in Holmes' new shopping-mall branches at suburban Lakeside and Oakwood shopping centers.

Canal Street to the other, and the stores did have a personality. And they had very loyal personnel. So you made wonderful relationships, from the cosmetics ladies to the buyers to the floorwalkers. Certain stores had certain things they specialized in, like Marks Isaacs had a great shoe-repair department and a wonderful ladies room. The ladies room, or as it was called, the ladies lounge, was certainly a place where mothers socialized. They had maybe a cup of water from the water fountain, kind of caught their breath before they walked to the next store.

Q: What kind of amenities did Holmes offer to shoppers?

A: People would arrive a bit earlier since with public transportation you never quite knew when you were getting there. At the store's Canal Street entrance, they would serve coffee in demitasse cups. It was just a kind of courtesy. There were so many courtesies extended to clients, and it was a nice way to socialize and soften up your entry into the store. Southern hospitality. And then on Saturday, they'd often have piano players. And that was a big thing because Saturday shopping was very important, and still is.

Q: Where did you meet friends on Canal Street?

A: Under the clock at D. H. Holmes, of course.

Q: Did you have a favorite department at D. H. Holmes?

A: The cosmetics department was always fascinating. The ladies who sold cosmetics were almost like celebrity greeters at Holmes and the other department stores. They had beautiful personalities and wonderful style. They were celebrities.

Q: Tell me about the sales clerks.

A: You definitely had your special ladies that you would visit. Even down to bringing them a little treat. And if you were really good friends, you might get invited to the employee cafeteria on their break.

Q: Now, you actually worked at Holmes.

A: When I was in high school I worked on what they called the "flying squad," filling in for employees who were sick or on vacation. So I was working in the candy department one day. They didn't necessarily train us for every department. You just had to pop in and act smart. So somebody wanted to buy

Gloria Scott was a sales representative for Revlon Cosmetics at D. H. Holmes Department Store on Canal Street for almost twenty years. (Courtesy of Peggy Scott Laborde)

Even more ambitious during its history on Canal Street was Maison Blanche. Its original home in the Mercier Building and the neighboring Grand Opera House were demolished, and between 1906 and 1909 they were replaced with what was then one of the city's tallest and finest skyscrapers. It housed the five-story department store, as well as floors of office space—home for many of downtown's doctors, dentists, and optometrists. Beginning in the 1920s, it also housed WSMB Radio on the top floor, where visitors could sit in front of a window in the studio and see announcers such as Nut and Jeff.

There were two tall radio towers atop the building during the late 1920s and 1930s. During construction the department store did not close, since the back wing of the new building was constructed first, while the store continued to operate from the Mercier Building. The store then moved into the new wing. The twenty-year-old Mercier Building was torn down to allow completion of the Canal Street portion of the new building, which the store moved into in 1909. Just like Holmes, Maison Blanche absorbed adjoining buildings, and in the 1920s both stores spread from the rear across Iberville Street. Maison Blanche, Holmes, and Krauss all had passageways over Iberville Street connecting their annexes.

Some of Canal Street's anchors found it more expedient to move to new quarters rather than expand. Stores moved around with fashion, and this was true on Canal Street where one block could be the difference between upscale and downscale. One such store was Godchaux's, which was founded by Leon Godchaux in 1840 from a peddler's cart. For many

One of two Woolworth's variety, or "dime," stores on Canal Street. Located at the corner of Canal and North Rampart streets, the store was built in the late 1930s and had an Art Deco facade. Famous for its bakery, it closed in the late 1990s. (Photo by Charles Franck; courtesy of The Historic New Orleans Collection)

A Woolworth's window display, photographed by Charles L. Franck Photographers. Variety stores such as Woolworth's were frequented by young people who often spent their limited allowances there on trips to Canal Street. (Courtesy of The Historic New Orleans Collection)

A view of the North Rampart and Canal Woolworth's shortly before it closed. (Courtesy of WYES-TV)

almond bark candy. So I'm putting the candy in a little box. I took her money and about five minutes later she came back. She said I'd given her the plastic almond bark. I didn't know there was display candy. She cracked her dentures. I feared for loss of my job! By the way, Holmes also had wonderful pastries. At the end of the workday they would discount the pastries for the employees so they could all take home a little treat. That's the kind of family store they were.

Q: Do you have memories of Krauss Department Store?

A: Krauss had the wooden floors, the old-time escalator from the 1939 New York World's Fair, the pneumatic tube system to handle credit purchases. If you sewed, you had to go to Krauss. There was also the Original and the Yardstick stores. So Krauss was at one end of Canal and those stores were on the other. Fabric was a big thing in the '40s and '50s because so many women sewed then.

Q: What about eating on Canal Street? Where would you grab a quick bite?

A: Well, I can remember Kress. It also had nice wooden floors. They sort of creaked, so you felt like you had to walk slowly and softly. But you could have a piece of apple pie and a coke or cup of coffee for a quarter, and that was a big treat.

Q: Special occasions like Community Bargain Days?

A: Well, it happened in August, and I believe in January. August was especially important because of *back-to-school business, but the cadence of Canal Street was just unbelievable. There was a coupon for a free bus ride. People came out en masse to shop.*

Q: What about shopping for Easter?

A: Easter was very special because New Orleans is such a Catholic city. You needed an Easter dress, and all the ladies wore hats. You either got white or black patent shoes for spring, and the first time you wore them was for the Easter holidays.

Q: The smells of some of the dime stores?

A: In Woolworth's you could always smell the nuts as soon as you walked in the door. I can also faintly remember plastic smells as the stores started selling more goods made with plastic.

Q: Weren't stores open later on Thursday?

A: Thursday night was the first night stores were open, and then Sears invented the Monday night opening. Stores in New York were open both evenings.

Q: Where else did you work and shop?

A: I worked from Krauss all the way down to Labiche's, and also Goldring's, Gus Mayer, Kreeger's, Maison Blanche, Holmes, and Godchaux's. For shopping, you had Keller-Zander and Imperial for shoes. You also had chain shoe stores such as Allen's, Baker's. If you couldn't afford a fancy dress, there

years the store was on Canal Street near Chartres Street. Then in 1892 a large, six-story "skyscraper-style" store was built at the corner of Chartres Street, where Godchaux's remained until 1926.

By then the corner was out of fashion, and the store moved to another early high-rise, Macheca's Imperial Building, built in 1902 between Carondelet and Baronne streets—which was then the center of the most upscale Canal Street shopping. Godchaux's remained at that location until its demise in the late 1980s, and until that time it was regarded as one of best stores in New Orleans. The Macheca Building is still around, although the Godchaux Building at Chartres Street, long an office building famous for housing Abe's Pawn Shop, was demolished in 1969 for the Marriott Hotel.

Kreeger's, a women's store born on Magazine Street in 1865 as an accessories and glove shop, moved to Canal Street near the corner of Bourbon Street by the 1890s. It expanded and remained there until it moved to Canal Place where it went out of business in the mid-1980s.

In 1900 another women's store, Gus Mayer, opened next door to D. H. Holmes. It grew to become a premier name in women's fashion not only in New Orleans but in several other southern cities as well. In 1949 Gus Mayer moved into a new building at the corner of Carondelet Street where it conducted business until its closure in the late 1980s. The Gus

A beautiful new store was built for Gus Mayer about 1950 at the corner of Carondelet in the heart of Canal Street's shopping area. It closed in the late 1980s. (Courtesy of The Historic New Orleans Collection)

Gus Mayer clothing store used a clover as its logo. A clover-shaped form was incorporated in the store's ceiling in the building it occupied at Carondelet Street from about 1950 until it closed in the late 1980s. (Courtesy of The Historic New Orleans Collection)

Mayer store is now long gone, but the name, initials, and cloverleaf logo remain prominently carved in the building constructed for the store.

Retail and fashion trends go hand in hand. They change frequently and dramatically, and throughout the years the look of Canal Street changed right along with fashion. At one time cast-iron galleries graced practically every building in the shopping district. Beginning in the 1850s, cast-ironwork became all the rage in New Orleans, and while most associated it with the French Quarter, it was just as common along Canal Street.

Not only was the ironwork attractive, but it protected pedestrians from the sun and rain. One of its first uses was on the Touro Block, which was ringed with ironwork galleries. By the end of the nineteenth century, ironwork galleries along Canal Street were going out of fashion, and they were being pulled off buildings.

Just as stores such as Godchaux's moved to better locations, others, including Holmes in 1912, rebuilt their facades, and from decade to decade few storefronts remained unchanged. While the upper floors of the Maison Blanche building barely changed, from the time the store opened in 1909 until it closed in the 1990s its show windows and doorways were redesigned every decade or so.

D. H. Holmes went from Tudor Gothic of the late 1840s to glazed terra cotta of the early twentieth century to shopping-mall modern of the

Many national and regional chain stores could be found along Canal Street, including Three Sisters.

was Mangel's, Three Sisters, Mayfair, Lord's. A nice level of stores that would allow you to put things on layaway, in which you'd pay a certain amount weekly or monthly or when your budget allowed.

So that helped a lot of working girls, because if you worked in a store, you couldn't just dress any way you wanted. When I first started working for Holmes in the '60s, I was just in high school. I was making ninety cents an hour. I had to provide myself with a black, brown, navy, gray, or dark-green dress or suit with shoes, sleeves, high heels, and hose every day. So if you couldn't afford to buy something in the store you worked for, you would put together a wardrobe in one of the less expensive stores, or perhaps make your own, because many of the stores had fabric departments.

Q: Tell me about how stores tried to encourage new shoppers.

A: Well, once you came to Canal Street and were a real junkie, you

Canal Street clothing store fashion coordinators such as Gus Mayer employee Rosalee Baker, center, served as role models for many New Orleans teenage girls. (Photo courtesy of Rosalee Baker)

really looked for a way to become part of the families in these stores. The stores were very smart. They looked at this Baby Boom group and one by one, starting with Kreeger's, developed groups for young people to participate in. They'd do seminars on public speaking. All kinds of things, modeling, anything to enhance this young clientele.

Kreeger's started something called the Mademoiselle K Club. Godchaux's had the Godchaux's Young Towners Club, and Holmes had the Young Circle Club. Maison Blanche had the Charmers Club, and they always hired a wonderful role model for you in each of these stores. They really influenced me. I knew them all, and I became friends and still am friends with some of them. They gave me such basic foundations in retail I can't even imagine.

Can you imagine giving someone five-feet-two the confidence

mid-1960s. Show windows along the street became larger and more numerous, and stone and brass replaced old-fashioned wooden window surrounds. During the Roaring Twenties, stores such as Stevens men's store and Haan's shoe store were redesigned with sleek Art Deco facades, helping give Canal Street the look of New York's Fifth Avenue and Chicago's State Street.

In the 1940s Walgreens, only a few years old at the time, had its Art Deco facade embellished with its still-distinctive neon lighting. In 1913 the national dime-store chain S. H. Kress arrived on Canal Street, next door to Maison Blanche, in a structure that was originally designed to be a motion picture theater. In the 1960s Kress added a red and white facade in an attempt to look modern; however, the building was returned to its original appearance in the 1990s when it was joined to the Maison Blanche building as part of the Ritz-Carlton Hotel.

Rubenstein Brothers, initially housed in one building near the corner of St. Charles Street, eventually expanded to include five buildings, some of which are among the oldest structures still standing on Canal Street; Rubenstein's ground floor show windows, however, are more modern in design and do not necessarily evoke the Victorian look of the upper floors.

Rubenstein Brothers is one of the few old-time local stores still operating on Canal Street. A block away near Carondelet Street is Coleman Adler's Jewelers, still in operation. These are the exceptions, as modern national retailing styles have changed. Few old names have been able to survive on Canal Street, which during its long history has seen many names come and go.

The corner of Canal and St. Charles as seen from the ironwork gallery of 633 Canal around 1868. By this time, the area was the center of the retail district, and cast-iron galleries were becoming common throughout the area. (Courtesy of The Historic New Orleans Collection)

Walgreens drugstore's Art Deco sign dates from the 1940s.

they could model? But they did and it wasn't just modeling. They had you spray customers with perfume. I worked every Saturday, from the time I was eleven years old. The most I ever got paid on Saturday for doing this and for modeling was a $2 gift certificate. But I would have done it for anything to be part of the family. It was wonderful. Then from the high school clubs the stores gradually developed college fashion boards. Maison Blanche and D. H. Holmes were very competitive.

And Godchaux's had the most fabulous fashion show. They did it every August, and they would have it on a Sunday, when the store was closed—all seven floors—show over 100 ensembles, shoes, hats, everything back-to-school, dogs on the runway. Rose Mouton would organize this show, and it was absolutely the best. And Maison Blanche would do a big fashion show in the spring, usually around their fragrance department. They would bring in people like Jean Shrimpton [an internationally known model at the time] and do a big fashion show with Yardley. I can remember having to go on the runway with a green mask on my face!

Q: Hat shops, where could you buy a nice hat?

A: All of the department stores had hats. And some even had two departments. Maison Blanche had one on the first floor and another on the second floor. The Better Hats departments would be on the second floor, because, of course, on the first floor they would get handled a lot and perhaps soiled. My Aunt Alice taught me how make hats. She was a milliner and worked for a time at D. H. Holmes and also sold gloves. And, of course, you wore a hat and gloves when you went to Canal Street.

Q: Any final thoughts about Canal Street?

A. What an amazing place. Looking in all the windows. The people who designed the windows were really stars. They were like set designers. They had such vision, and we couldn't wait for the changes and, of course, the holiday windows. At night, to walk, go to the movies, and see what was in the windows of the stores—it was a delight.

Along with shops such as Holmes, Maison Blanche, Gus Mayer, Kreeger's, Marks Isaacs, Goldring's, L&L Furs, Hausmann's, and Rapp's Luggage Store of more recent memory, earlier names such as Danziger's, Schwarz, Marx Brothers, Fellman's, Fiebleman's, Mayer Israel, and Keller-Zander pop up only in old photos and postcards of the thoroughfare.

Occasional fires altered the face of Canal Street. In 1892 a spectacular blaze leveled several hundred feet of stores on either side of Bourbon Street, including several of the Touro Buildings on the Quarter side, while on the lake side Kreeger's was consumed and the fire barely missed D. H. Holmes. Considered some of the most valuable retail space in town, the sites were quickly rebuilt, but there was no attempt to match what had been lost. The new buildings were thoroughly 1890s in style, with ornate cornices and window detailing very different from those built in earlier years.

In 1903 the Imperial Shoe Store moved into the building on the corner of Bourbon Street, and eventually Kreeger's occupied the buildings across Bourbon. Both stores ceased business in the 1980s. Next door to Imperial a large five-story building was occupied by the Schwarz Dry Goods Store. By the 1920s this became one of several F. W. Woolworth

Workrooms were often located on the upper floors of Canal Street businesses. This jewelry workroom, with skylight, was at Coleman Adler's Jewelry Store circa 1912. (Courtesy of The Historic New Orleans Collection)

Rubenstein Brothers Men's Store embraces five of the earliest buildings on Canal Street.

Adler's Jewelry Store opened on Canal Street in 1898. Its ornate clock became the store's symbol.

Several stores were located at the corner of Bourbon Street in the 1950s, including Kreeger's Women's Store and the Imperial Shoe Store. (Courtesy of The Historic New Orleans Collection)

While there were a few men's stores on Canal Street, including Rubenstein Brothers and Stevens, during the 1940s and 1950s, most of the stores, such as the Polly Shop in the Audubon Building, catered to women.

five and dime stores on the French Quarter side of Canal Street. Another was in the Audubon Building in the early 1920s, and a third one was built in 1938 at the corner of North Rampart Street. In 1949 the Bourbon Street Woolworth building was torn down and replaced by a sleek, modern store that operated until the demise of the Woolworth chain in the 1990s. This building in its turn was demolished for the Astor Crown Plaza Hotel, which was designed to interpret the 1890s building that had been torn down a half-century earlier.

The surviving center portion of the Touro Block became Marks Isaacs Department Store, but with its closure in the 1960s the site was altered to suit new store tenants. In 2002 the property became the Alexa (now Astor Crown Plaza) Hotel, which has a close facsimile of the old Marks Isaacs facade. Only three buildings of the Touro Block remain near the corner of Royal Street, now minus the wide iron-work gallery that had once graced them.

In 1900 the seven-story "skyscraper" Morris Building, built in the late 1880s at the corner of Camp Street, burned down to its third floor along

To help provide a better fit, an x-ray machine was used at shoe stores such as Imperial on Canal Street. (Courtesy of the Museum of Questionable Medical Devices)

with an adjoining Canal Street building. The Morris Building was repaired, with the addition of its distinctive bay windows and a cornice that is no longer there. Its neighbor was rebuilt where Rapp's Luggage Store was once located.

Directly across Canal Street from the Touro Block, a spectacular fire in 1908 burned out the middle of the row of buildings that once included the former J. Levois and Jamison building. As with the other fire sites, this retail space was too valuable to go vacant for very long and new buildings were quickly built.

As Canal Street was the center of the luxury trade, it was only logical that some of the finest examples of the city's jewelry, gold, silver, and china were sold in its stores. and the shop windows revealed that all that glitters is indeed not always gold. Here, goods were both imported and manufactured on the premises in the shops' own workrooms. Among the largest and finest in the mid-nineteenth century was the shop of Hyde and Goodrich in the Touro Block at the corner of Royal Street, where a large carved pelican attached to the gallery corner identified the store. In 1865 Hyde and Goodrich became A. B. Griswold, which operated on Canal Street until it was taken over by Hausmann's in 1924.

Hausmann's operated in the 700 block of Canal Street until it was absorbed by an out-of-town jeweler and the Canal Street store was closed in the 1980s. For years Hausmann's near neighbor was Coleman Adler's, which was established in 1898 and remains one of the handful of old Canal Street retailers still in business. Other jewelers such as A. M. Hill, F. A. Tyler, Greger and Wilson, C. H. Zimmermann, Maurice Schooler, Miller Brothers, and White Brothers were long time residents of Canal Street that are now long gone. Also gone are the national jewelry chains such as Zale's and Gordon's, which have migrated to shopping malls.

Canal Street has long been a center of entertainment, not only for New Orleans but for much of the South. By far the largest and most important southern city until well into the twentieth century, it was a leading retail center as well. Its rich music tradition, including a fondness for opera as well as a unique jazz heritage, made it the center of a large regional market for instruments and sheet music.

Philip Werlein owned one of the most important music stores in the South. Established in 1842, Werlein's had several Canal Street locations, including the Touro Block, until 1904 when the store moved into a new building on Canal Street near Chartres Street. The store closed around 1990 and the structure currently houses the Palace Cafe. Werlein's was a leading publisher of sheet music, its most famous being the song "Dixie," published in 1860.

Another music publisher with a shop on Canal Street, and for a while in the Touro Block, was Grunewald's, which eventually relocated to Baronne Street, where the company stayed in business until the 1960s. Still another publisher, A. E. Blackmar, operated on Canal Street between Burgundy and North Rampart streets in the 1860s and 1870s. The publisher of the Confederate song "The Bonnie Blue Flag," Blackmar moved to San Francisco in 1876.

Along with being publishers, all of these music stores operated sales rooms. There were, however, other music stores that specialized only in the sale of pianos and other instruments. M. Elie, a piano seller, operated in conjunction with the publisher Blackmar. From 1880 to 1920,

The facade of Werlein's was preserved when the former music store became the Palace Cafe. (Photo by Kerri McCaffety)

Music and Musical Instruments at

Grunewald's Music House, 127 Canal,

Grunewald Hall, 18 Baronne Street, New Orleans.

Pianos and Organs at

This trade card advertisement is for Louis Grunewald's Music Store. Grunewald built the Grunewald Hotel, which would evolve first into the Roosevelt and then into today's Fairmont Hotel.

LOUIS GRUNEWALD,

GENERAL AGENT FOR THE

Leading Pianos of the World.

STEINWAY, PLEYEL, WEBER, KNABE,

SOLD ON EASY MONTHLY PAYMENTS.

OLD PIANOS REPAIRED OR TAKEN IN EXCHANGE.

Grunewald Hall, 18 Baronne St.,

AND 127 CANAL STREET,

NEW ORLEANS, LA.

New Orleans had its own "Tin Pan Alley," with music stores that also published songs. In addition to Grunewald's, other establishments were Junius Hart and A. E. Blackmar. (Courtesy of Peggy Scott Laborde)

Junius Hart was strictly a piano seller in a building ringed with ironwork at the corner of Burgundy Street. As player pianos, gramophones, and radios began to fill the family home, many music stores similar to Hart's were forced out of business. Werlein's, by adding phonograph records, phonographs, and radios to its inventory, was better able to compete through most of the twentieth century, and was patronized by virtually every musician and music lover in the city.

Few people remember the days when shoppers did not carry their purchases home. Daniel Holmes pioneered in the delivery of customers'

HOLMES

The D. H. Holmes logo consisted of the company's intertwined initials. It was in use for over a century, although periodically the style of lettering was changed to fit more contemporary tastes. (Courtesy of Peggy Scott Laborde)

goods, and soon virtually everything, no matter how small, was being delivered. By the mid-twentieth century this was changing, however, as buyers often carried their own packages home in store bags. Distinctive store bags were provided by just about every store, and in their individual styles, the bags became another way of advertising.

At one time everyone knew when a shopper had made a purchase at Maison Blanche, for example, because he or she carried deep-green bags with views of famous New Orleans sites. Godchaux's and Krauss also showed New Orleans views on their bags. Holmes' bags were either blue or tan and announced that the store was "Louisiana's Quality Department Store." MB (Maison Blanche) was the "Greatest Store South."

"Let's meet under the clock at Holmes" and various derivatives were commonly heard in the downtown New Orleans shopping district during much of the twentieth century. (Photo by C. F. Weber; courtesy of Bergeron Gallery)

In the days before bank credit cards, some stores distributed their own. In New Orleans a white and orange shopper's card was used by several stores, including Holmes, Maison Blanche, and Godchaux's. The card lasted from the 1960s until the closure of most of these stores in the 1980s.

Although D. H. Holmes had a narrow frontage along Canal Street, its designers made good use of the interior space, which encompassed nearly a city block. This 1951 photograph shows typical window displays that greeted shoppers. (Courtesy of The Historic New Orleans Collection)

This bird's-eye view of part of the first floor of D. H. Holmes in the 1950s shows the department store's expansive floor space. (Photo by C. F. Weber; courtesy of Bergeron Gallery)

Gindy's, at 1030 Canal, was one of many camera, electronic, and gift stores operated by Julius Gindi from the mid-1950s until the 1970s. According to Gindi's family, it was he who introduced transistor radios to New Orleans. (Courtesy of Francine Gindi Segal)

There were also logos with which everybody was familiar. From the late nineteenth century D. H. Holmes used its intertwined initials, which were redesigned periodically. Gus Mayer had bright yellow bags with a green cloverleaf, while Kreeger's had gray bags with a large ornate "K." Bags from Stevens, Adler's, Hausmann's, Goldring's, and a multitude of other stores told everybody where a shopper had been. Except for a few stores such as Adler's and Rubenstein Brothers, the store bags now seen on Canal Street are from national chains such as Saks Fifth Avenue, Brooks Brothers, Gucci, and the Pottery Barn,

Some old stores were noted for their services. At Holmes, there were departments for shoe repair and optical and hearing needs, and even a drug counter. The store was also noted for its liberal return policy. Even worn shoes were accepted as returns. By the 1970s adhering to this policy proved challenging, and sometimes impossible. Some residents remember the time a woman tried to return a worn-looking wig that she had washed and dried in her microwave oven.

Photography was introduced to New Orleans in 1839. From its earliest days, there have been photographers with studios on Canal Street making

Washburn   NEGATIVES PRESERVED   111 Canal St. NEW ORLEANS.

From the mid-1800s, photography studios were often located on the upper floors of Canal Street retail establishments. Pictured here is the work of William W. Washburn, one of the most noted portrait photographers in New Orleans in the mid-nineteenth century. (Courtesy of Peggy Scott Laborde)

This carte-de-visite was a small paper photograph mounted on a card that became common after the Civil War. Photographer Eugene Simon was also a visual artist.

family portraits and documenting weddings, confirmations, graduations, and other milestones of life. Photographers often moved from studio to studio, and while there were studios all over town, there were a number of important photographers who were associated for many years with Canal Street.

The Moses family of photographers was located at the corner of Camp Street from the 1850s into the early twentieth century, and the noted Theodore Lilienthal had an address near Chartres Street from the 1860s into the 1890s. Of more recent memory, Richard Relf worked at various locations on Canal Street around Royal and Bourbon during the first decades of the twentieth century. Several other photographers could also be found there. For many a young person in New Orleans, dressing up and going to Canal Street sometimes meant having one's picture taken.

Sidewalks are an important asset to any successful shopping district, and the wide pedestrian walkways of the "Great Wide Way" were able to

Having one's photograph taken was often part of the downtown Canal Street shopping experience, particularly for special occasions, such as to commemorate this little boy's first communion in the 1880s.

The heart of the wholesale hardware district on Canal between Camp and Magazine in the 1870s. The Sheraton New Orleans Hotel now fills this block. (Courtesy of The Historic New Orleans Collection)

accommodate the large crowds necessary to maintain an array of big shops before the automobile altered shopping patterns in the twentieth century.

In its earliest days, Canal Street was little more than just a very wide and not very long dirt path, and even as it grew, the possibility of a navigation canal down its middle limited any incentive to adequately pave it. As townhouses and businesses proliferated along its route, some attempts at beautification began to materialize. By the 1830s rows of sycamore trees graced the neutral ground. By the 1850s the roadway was a patchwork of various paving materials such as cobblestone and brick, but in other spots it was in near ruin. Furthermore, the sycamores between Carondelet Street and the Mississippi River were gone.

All of the sidewalks were paved with flagstones by the 1840s, but they, too, were in disrepair and uneven. Man-made drainage was virtually non-existent. Rainwater found its own level and usually formed little rivulets that crisscrossed the median. Making matters worse, the median

S. H. Kress was part of a large national chain and was an important part of the Canal Street shopping scene from its opening in the early 1910s until its demise about seventy years later. This is one of its displays for hams and Easter purses in 1955. (Photograph by Charles L. Franck Photographers; courtesy of The Historic New Orleans Collection)

had become a dumping ground for old barrels, wagon wheels, sugar kettles, and scrap of all kinds—all this along what was the richest and most fashionable shopping street in the South.

When Judah Touro—developer of the Touro Block—died in 1854, his will provided funds to improve Canal Street. Not until 1859 was this work finally carried out. Massive square granite stones were used for paving the roadway; sidewalks were widened and leveled; gutters with granite sides were installed along both the sidewalks and the neutral ground to drain off rainwater. The neutral ground was also enclosed with chains supported by small iron posts. At last Canal Street was befitting of its position, and the *Daily Picayune* declared that the thoroughfare "promised to be the place of beauty and fashion of the city." To honor Judah Touro, the city council voted to name the street Touro Boulevard. Public opinion and tradition prevailed, however, and people continued to call the street Canal. In 1855 it was officially named Canal Street.

Maintenance was often a difficult task, especially in the city's financially strapped years after the Civil War. Poor soil conditions often left the sidewalk flagstones cracked and wobbly, while granite stones along the driveways were uneven, sometimes causing wagons to become stuck between the stones. Walking on the stones could squeeze water and mud between them and up onto shoes and skirt hems of female pedestrians.

Drainage was a special problem, and the deep gutters—which were usually filled with litter—were hardly able to manage the runoff of rainwater at times. Water from a heavy summer shower could easily back up

Window shopping on Canal Street was a popular pastime, and window displays could be imaginative, as evidenced by this display for undergarments at Lord's Women's Store at the corner of Baronne. (Photograph by Charles L. Franck Photographers; courtesy of The Historic New Orleans Collection)

The block of Canal Street between St. Charles and Carondelet in 1899. Of note is the photographic studio of Gustave Moses & Son, a family of Canal Street photographers who had studios at the corner of Camp Street beginning in the 1850s. The buildings shown here were replaced after a large fire in 1908. (Courtesy of The Historic New Orleans Collection)

onto the sidewalks and into stores. Shoppers sometimes had to sit on counters until the flood water subsided. The gutters, which were crossed by stone or cast-iron foot bridges, could also be dangerous, since they became slippery when wet. It was not unheard of for people to accidentally slip into a gutter.

By the 1880s, most people constantly complained about the condition of Canal Street's paving. There was a proposal in the mid-1880s to pave the street with asphalt as far as Claiborne Avenue and to provide it with subsurface drainage. Asphalt had been successfully used to pave St. Charles Avenue, but the St. Charles paving project, along with the subsequent paving of one mile of Baronne Street downtown, had taken such a great amount of time that merchants successfully resisted any improvement to Canal Street at the time for fear of losing too much business.

In 1899—the same year New Orleans voters approved of the city's most far-reaching drainage, sewerage, and waterworks plan in its history—Canal Street underwent its first full-scale beautification in four decades. Asphalt replaced the old granite paving blocks, subsurface drains replaced the open gutters, and new electric light standards were erected. By that time Canal Street was such a popular shopping destination that work was kept to a fairly tight schedule to insure that business was not too adversely affected.

In the days before canned music, some stores had bands, piano players, and organs. Here, Edward Larmann plays the organ at S. H. Kress. (Courtesy of the family of Edward Larmann)

A portion of this vast repaving project took place in February 1899 when Carnival weekend coincided with the city's worst freeze ever recorded. In spite of this, all the parades, except for Proteus, which was postponed, managed to roll among broken paving stones and over frozen mud. On Mardi Gras night, as the thaw was setting in, throngs of revelers poured into Canal Street to welcome the Mistick Krewe of Comus, see the spectacle of brightly lighted buildings, and celebrate into the night as usual.

With the advent of the twentieth century, a newly paved and brightly illuminated Canal Street truly came of age, a symbol of a new and progressive century. Thirty years later, Canal Street underwent another complete revamping from the river to Claiborne Avenue. For twenty blocks new foundations and asphalt were laid. The sidewalks were paved with red and white terrazzo. It was lovely to look at but slippery when wet and a hazard for anyone walking along Canal Street until about 1984. Tall, ornamented light standards, which are still in use, were erected, and bear emblems honoring the various nations that have governed New Orleans.

By the early 1950s office buildings generated more activity on Canal

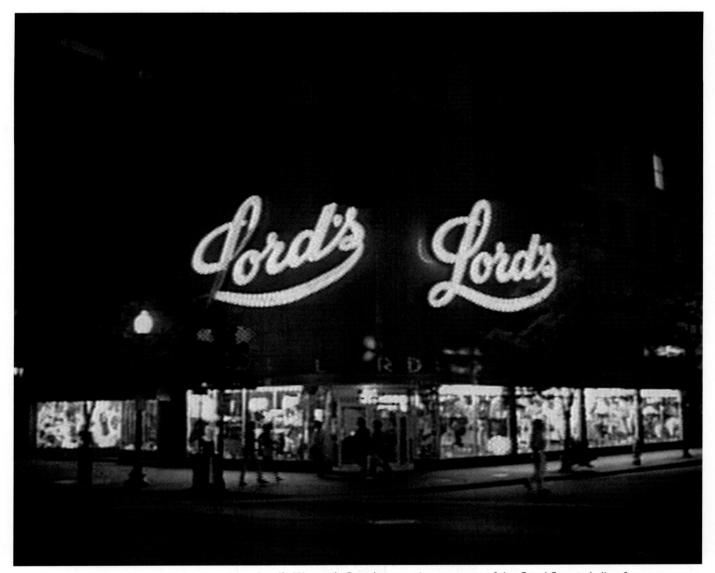

Lord's Women's Store's neon sign was part of the Canal Street skyline for many years.

Street. The Texaco Oil Company's local high-rise headquarters was built across Marais Street from the Wirth Building in 1954. Texaco, however, moved its headquarters into a new skyscraper on Poydras Street in the 1980s. Since then the building has been used for various purposes.

Several other oil exploration companies set up office in this area during the 1950s and 1960s. There was the Art Deco Esso Building not far from the Joy Theatre, while half a block away on Elk Place was the Gulf Building, which was formerly the Elks Club. All of the oil companies had local tour offices where a collector of highway and city maps could always acquire new additions for his collection. There were also the 1960s high-rise Odeco and Tidewater Marine buildings, now used by the University of New Orleans and Tulane University, respectively. This section continues to develop as a series of offices connected to the growing medical complex nearby.

The character of shopping on Canal Street has changed. Gone are the large locally owned department stores. Most of the high-end shopping is now concentrated toward the river end on Canal, especially the Canal Place Shopping Center. Elsewhere, shops that sell inexpensive shoes, souvenirs, and electronic gadgets keep locals hoping for better days.

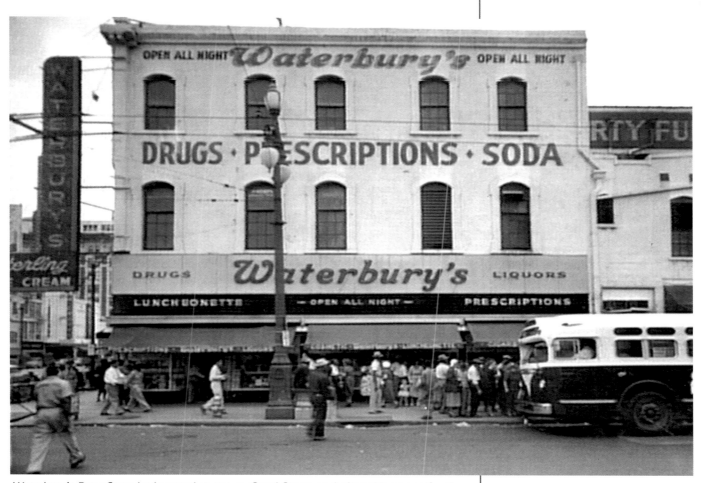

Waterbury's Drug Store had several stores on Canal Street, including this one at South Rampart, during the 1940s and 1950s. The building has housed Fischer's Jewelry Store since 1962. (Courtesy of The Historic New Orleans Collection)

The Grand Opera House was an outgrowth of the Varieties Theater and was home of the ball of the Mistick Krewe of Comus during the late nineteenth century. Its site is now occupied by part of the Ritz-Carlton Hotel. (Courtesy of The Historic New Orleans Collection)

CHAPTER THREE
That's Entertainment

OPERA, LIVE THEATRE, and concerts have long been a part of the New Orleans cultural scene. Canal Street became a part of the theater tradition in 1871 when the Varieties Theater opened next door to Christ Church, between Dauphine and Burgundy streets. The entrance to the theater was through one of the buildings of Union Terrace, a row of three Greek Revival townhouses built in 1833. Not successful as residences, they were soon converted to commercial uses. The Varieties was born as the Gaiety Theater on Gravier Street that burned and was moved to Canal Street.

In the early 1870s, part of Union Terrace also burned, leaving only the Varieties entrance. The theater, which had one of the finest stairways in the South, was renovated and enlarged in 1881 and renamed the Grand Opera House. Illustrious stars of the day who performed there included

One of the finest staircases in New Orleans was in the lobby of the Grand Opera House. This elegant feature was used to advantage by the various Mardi Gras krewes, including the Mistick Krewe of Comus, which once staged its annual ball here. (Courtesy of The Historic New Orleans Collection)

In Astonishing Feats of

Mind Reading and Mental Phenomena

Next week — WALKER WHITESIDE in
Tragedy.

VITASCOPE HALL

Cor. Canal and Exchange Place.

All New Pictures Again This Week

Still all the rage and cynosure of all eyes of
Amusement Lovers,

Admission 10 cents.

Doors open 10 a. m. to 5 p. m., and from 6 to
10 p. m.

WAINWRIGHT & ROCK,
Sole Owners and Managers.
X Rays at Vitascope Hall.

LAST EXCURSION.

Vitascope Hall, located on the corner of Exchange Place and Canal, is reputed by some to have been the oldest movie theater in the United States. It was certainly among the earliest.

Busy crowds are seen at the corner of North Rampart Street in 1942. This side door to the Saenger Theatre became the entrance of the Saenger-Orleans in 1964. (Courtesy of The Historic New Orleans Collection)

Sarah Bernhardt, Joseph Jefferson, and Edwin Booth (brother of Abraham Lincoln's assassin, John Wilkes Booth).

The Grand Opera House, like most theaters of the day, did not serve as just a theater, but could be converted to a ballroom. It vied with the French Opera House as home to several Carnival balls, including the Mistick Krewe of Comus. It was torn down in 1906 to make way for an expanded Maison Blanche.

Although Canal Street did not dominate live theater, it became the center of New Orleans' first-run movie trade for almost three-quarters of a century. During the early twentieth century, motion pictures were replacing live theater as a chief form of American entertainment, and this was as true in New Orleans as elsewhere. Reputedly, although rather debatably, the first motion picture theater in the United States was Vitascope Hall, which opened on June 26, 1896, at the corner of Canal Street and Exchange Place in a no longer-extant building that was ringed with ironwork at the time.

The theater existed for only a short time. By the 1910s there were several movie theaters along Canal Street, such as the Alamo, near North Rampart Street, the Plaza, near Dauphine, and the Dreamworld, near St. Charles.

The city's first modest movie palace was the Trianon, which opened in 1912 a few doors from Carondelet Street. In 1914 the Tudor opened between Camp and St. Charles streets, and four years later the Globe opened next door. Both theaters were among the grandest in the city when they opened, and for a number of years were among the city's cadre of first-run houses, cementing Canal Street's role as the home of the first-run picture houses. By World War II both theaters had been relegated to second-run status, and at the time they both closed in the early 1960s they specialized in fairly low-grade fare. The J. W. Marriott Hotel (formerly Le Meridien Hotel) now occupies those sites.

Built in the 1910s, the Globe Theater and its newer neighbor the Tudor Theater were on the site where the J. W. Marriott Hotel now stands. They were first-run theaters during the 1920s, but were overshadowed by bigger, grander Canal Street movie palaces that were built on Canal Street in the late 1920s. They ended their days as lower-grade theaters in the 1960s. (Courtesy of The Historic New Orleans Collection)

According to longtime New Orleans entertainment critic Al Shea, the Loew's State Theatre was the "Cadillac" of local movie theaters because it featured movies produced by Metro-Goldwyn-Mayer. This photo of a young moviegoer sitting in the ornate lobby was taken in 1938. (Courtesy of Rene Brunet)

During the Roaring Twenties, there were several movie houses along the street between Carondelet and South Rampart streets. They included the Newcomb and the Wonderland, next door. The Wonderland burned in 1935, and reopened the next year as the Center. By the 1960s it showed X-rated movies, but was renovated as the first-run Ciné Royale. The Ciné Royale, which eventually reverted to X-rated movies again, was demolished soon after 2000 to allow the expansion of a Walgreens drugstore.

The Orpheum Theater on University Place opened as a vaudeville house in 1920, but soon included movies as part of its program. While the Orpheum is not on Canal Street, it is only a few steps away from the two grand Canal Street movie palaces of the 1920s that stand across the street from each other. In 1926 the Loew's State Theatre opened, and like the Orpheum, began as a vaudeville house, but included movies on the

The Loew's State Theatre, when the movie Gone With the Wind *was playing, in January 1940. According to longtime movie theater operator Rene Brunet, as many as 90,000 people went to the Loew's in the course of a week to see the film. (Courtesy of Rene Brunet)*

Adding to the Canal Street skyline was the Loew's State Theatre sign. When the theater opened on April 3, 1926, entertainment included a film and a stage show. (Courtesy of Rene Brunet)

When the Loew's State Theatre opened in the mid-1920s, it offered both vaudeville performances and motion pictures. The theater provided an early form of air conditioning for the crowds of grateful patrons. (Courtesy of Rene Brunet)

On the South Rampart Street side of the Loew's State Theatre was an entrance for the black community. It was then referred to as the colored entrance. Seats were located in the balcony. This photo is from 1928, two years after the theater opened. (Courtesy of Rene Brunet)

The Krauss Department Store, the Southern Railway Station, and the La Salle Hotel dominated the area of Canal Street at Rampart, at right, in 1922. The Saenger Theatre was not yet built, and behind its future site can be seen several of the larger buildings of the Storyville red-light district, which had closed in 1917. (Courtesy of The Historic New Orleans Collection)

bill from the start. The Loew's was the largest movie theater in the city with 3,400 seats, and was home to the popular features of M-G-M. In 1935 *Naughty Marietta,* set in New Orleans, was shown there, and in January 1940 *Gone With the Wind* played for a number of weeks, a long run by the standards of the day.

Although planned in the early 1920s, the larger and more lavish Saenger Theatre did not open until 1927. After five years of design and construction, the theater, with its Mighty Morton organ that would rise from the side of the orchestra pit and its Florentine interior, opened with considerable hoopla. Like the Loew's State and the Orpheum, the Saenger attracted long lines for memorable movies into the 1970s.

Two additional, yet smaller, first-run theaters also opened on Canal Street. The Joy Theatre began at the corner of Elk Place in 1947. It was the most modern theater in New Orleans at the time, but was much less grandiose than the palatial Saenger and Loew's State. In 1964 the balcony of the Saenger was enclosed to become the jewel-like Saenger-Orleans. With head rests and stadium seating before such things were

Part of the Loew's State and Saenger experience was listening to an organist perform before—and, in the early days, during—the showing of a film. Longtime movie theater operator Rene Brunet is shown here playing the Mighty Morton organ, still located on the side of the orchestra pit at the Saenger Theatre. (Photo courtesy of Rene Brunet)

The Joy Theatre, which opened in 1947, included a "crying room," a glass-enclosed area behind the back row that enabled parents with young children to enjoy the show without disturbing the other patrons. (Photo courtesy of Rene Brunet)

The facade of the Saenger Theatre was built in the early 1920s as part of the La Salle Hotel building. The theater itself was constructed a few years later. Note the angle parking along the median. (Courtesy of The Historic New Orleans Collection)

A view of the interior of the Saenger Theatre in its early days. (Photograph by Charles
L. Franck Photographers; courtesy of The Historic New Orleans Collection)

A cluster of bars was located on Canal Street during the 1950s at the
river end of the street and also past Rampart Street. In the latter
neighborhood, one of the more popular establishments was the Brass
Rail, seen here in 1952. As a teenager, singer/pianist Dr. John recalls
sneaking out of Mass at Sacred Heart of Jesus Roman Catholic Church
and hopping on the Canal streetcar to make the early Sunday morning set performed by rhythm and blues artist Paul Gayten and his
band. This club was known for its interracial bands at a time when it
was illegal for black and white musicians to perform together.
(Courtesy of The Historic New Orleans Collection)

A display at the Brass Rail in 1952, photographed by Charles L. Franck Photographers. This popular bar was near the Joy Theatre and not far from Elk Place. (Courtesy of The Historic New Orleans Collection)

common, the Saenger-Orleans was home to big-budget, long-run "road-show" features such as *My Fair Lady* and *The Sound of Music,* movies that in some places ran for years. Just as people dressed up to go shopping on Canal Street in the 1960s, people also wore their finery to their reserved seats at the Saenger-Orleans.

As first-run movies moved to the suburbs and multiplex venues, the old downtown theaters were either converted to other uses or left vacant. The Saenger-Orleans had only a short life of a little over ten years and closed with the Saenger in the mid-1970s. A few years later, the structure was converted into a live theater offering Broadway productions. Fortunately, its ceiling of "twinkling stars" remains intact, along with a cloud machine. The theater was damaged by Hurricane Katrina.

Movie fans need not totally despair. There's a multi-screen Landmark Cinema at the Canal Place shopping complex near the Mississippi riverfront. Even though the Golden Days of the silver screen are over for Canal Street (as with many of America's downtown main streets), movies are still being presented on the thoroughfare.

NEW ORLEANS' MOST FABULOUS COCKTAIL LOUNGE AND BAR

The **BRASS RAIL**

Lois Marie

★ "The Continentals," A Clever Foursome

★ Lois Marie's Golden Voice and Accordion

★ Jimmy Reagan, Irish Tenor and Pianist Supreme

Continuous entertainment to 3 a. m.

Reagan

DANCING — 1316 CANAL ST. — AIR CONDITIONED

In the 1950s, air conditioning was not common in New Orleans, and its availability in the Brass Rail warranted mention in an advertisement.

Although the St. Charles Hotel was not on Canal Street, it was only a block away, on St. Charles Street, and is visible here from the Henry Clay Monument in the late 1860s. Popular with visitors who came to New Orleans to shop, the first of three St. Charles hotels was built in the 1830s. The second structure, built in the 1850s, is shown here. It was an establishment that had survived fires and rebuilding only to be demolished in the early 1970s. The lot was vacant until the construction of the Place St Charles office building in the 1980s. The building on the left still stands as part of Rubenstein Brothers. (Courtesy of The Historic New Orleans Collection)

CHAPTER FOUR
Hotels

FROM ITS EARLIEST days when it was evolving into the main street of New Orleans, Canal Street has been the address of hotels, although it was not until the twentieth century that hotels would be a major part of its commerce.

In the 1830s there were several hotels on Canal Street near the river, and in most cases they were operated like boarding houses. Although hotels tend to offer short-term stays, it was not unusual at the time for some people to use a hotel as their homes.

Among the hotels on Canal Street were the Union Hotel and the Planters Hotel, located a few doors from each other between Tchoupitoulas and Magazine streets. They were housed in three-story row buildings that were typical of the commercial style then found through-out the city's commercial district. The Planters, undergoing repair work on its first floor that most likely weakened its structure, collapsed into a massive pile of rubble at 2 A.M. on May 15, 1835. Fifty of its guests were buried among the bricks and timber. Forty were rescued. The disaster brought crowds of sightseers, and the event garnered enough national attention to warrant a lithographed illustration by Nathaniel Currier.

Some of the grandest early hotels in the United States were in New Orleans—built during the city's glory days of the 1830s—but none of them were on Canal Street. In the French Quarter there was the St. Louis Hotel, which opened in 1836 on the site of today's Omni Royal Orleans. The St. Louis burned in 1841, but was immediately rebuilt. The St. Charles opened in 1842 on St. Charles Street between Common and Gravier. With its tall dome it must have offered a splendid view of Canal Street only one block away.

The St. Louis eventually fell on hard times and was torn down in 1916 after being vacant for two decades. The St. Charles, on the other hand, was successful from the start. It lasted through three incarnations, after having been destroyed twice by fire, until the early 1970s, when it was torn down. Its site is now occupied by the Place St. Charles skyscraper office building that towers over the low-rise buildings of nearby Canal Street.

Other nineteenth century hotels included the City Hotel and St. James Hotel on Camp Street and the Verandah Hotel, with its early use of cast-ironwork galleries diagonally across from the St. Charles Hotel. None of the big hotels were on Canal Street except for the Perry House. It was on

The Monteleone Hotel, visible here at the right about 1915, was originally called the Commercial. Hotels such as this one on Royal at Iberville streets were usually just off Canal Street. (Courtesy of The Historic New Orleans Collection)

the corner of Baronne Street during the 1850s and 1860s and replaced by the Chess, Checkers, and Whist Club. Since the 1930s it has been the site of a Walgreens drug store. The main portion of Canal Street was directed to the needs of shoppers and not those of visitors.

There were several late nineteenth and early twentieth century hotels just off Canal Street that counted among their guests people who came to town to shop on Canal. These hotels were near the back doors of some of the big stores. One of these was the Commercial Hotel on Royal and Iberville streets, which evolved into the Monteleone Hotel. A half block away in the 100 block of Royal Street was the Cosmopolitan Hotel—once called the Astor—which stretched for a full block back to Bourbon Street.

The Cosmopolitan was actually two hotel buildings connected by its restaurant. One of the buildings was for the family trade while the other was for traveling salesmen. A nearby hotel called La Louisiane on Iberville Street opened in 1880. For a long time there has been a restaurant with the same name on the hotel property. Also on Iberville Street, the Rendon opened at the corner of Dauphine Street. By the 1950s this had become the Hotel Senator, but following a fire it was replaced by the D. H. Holmes annex and parking garage.

One hotel not located on Canal was so close that it should be considered a Canal Street hotel. In the early 1890s the Grunewald Hotel opened on Baronne Street, half a block off Canal Street. It was built on the site of the music and theater venue Grunewald Hall by Louis Grunewald. He was owner of a music store once located in the Touro Block on Canal Street. His elegant six-story hotel was one of most luxurious in the city and had a sumptuous lobby and staircase.

This is the Roosevelt, now the Fairmont Hotel, as it appeared in the mid-1920s when it was the largest hotel in New Orleans. Part of the building had previously been the Grunewald. The massive, block-long buildings were visible from Canal Street, seen in the foreground of this image taken by Charles L. Franck Photographers. (Courtesy of The Historic New Orleans Collection)

In 1908 an annex was added to the Grunewald on University Place in what was then one of the tallest buildings in the city. In 1924 the old Baronne Street building was replaced with another tall addition, and at this point the hotel's name was changed to the Roosevelt. It remained the Roosevelt until the 1960s when it was acquired by the Fairmont chain and given its current name. Its massive, block-long building is so visible from Canal Street that it has been as important a part of the Canal Street panorama as any building on the street.

The 1920s saw an increase in the number of Canal Street hotels. The LaSalle Hotel, into which part of the Saenger Theatre was later incorporated, was conveniently located just a block from the Southern Railway Terminal on Basin Street. Two high-rise hotels opened on the opposite side of Canal Street at about the same time. The Hotel New Orleans, which was called the Marbeck for a while during the 1930s, currently operates as the Amerihost Inns and Suites. For a few years during the 1990s it served as a dormitory for the nearby Tulane Medical School.

With its popular rooftop ballroom, the Jung Hotel was the place to stay

The Hotel New Orleans opened in the early 1920s not far from the Southern Railway Terminal. It was once the tallest building on Canal Street. When this photograph was taken by Charles L. Franck Photographers about 1930, the hotel was called the Marbeck. (Courtesy of The Historic New Orleans Collection)

The Jung Hotel was built in the late 1920s and after several additions was among the largest hotels in New Orleans. Its rooftop was a popular dance and party spot.

during the 1920s. Several annexes were added to the hotel, now called the Park Plaza, making it one of the largest of the older hotels in the city. The nearby massive Claiborne Towers apartment building of the early 1950s has gone through several hotel conversions.

Few other hotels were added to Canal Street's hotel inventory in the years after the Depression of the 1930s, but with the growing convention industry in the 1960s, this began to change. Although a multi-story Governor House motor hotel was erected at the corner of South Claiborne in the mid-1960s, most of the development activity was closer to the riverfront. One of the first new 1960s hotels in this area was the International Hotel (today's DoubleTree Hotel), with its little triangle park facing Canal Street between Tchoupitoulas and South Peters streets.

In the late 1960s, virtually an entire block between Chartres and Dorsiere Place, including the old Godchaux's Building at Chartres Street, was leveled for the forty-two-story Marriott Hotel. It opened in 1972 as the city's tallest and most modern hotel. This was the same year that the city's tallest building, One Shell Square, opened on St. Charles near Poydras Street. In the early 1980s, the One Canal Place office building opened adjoining the tall Trusthouse Forte (for many years a Westin Hotel), sitting atop the parking garage at Canal Place. Today it is a Wyndham Hotel.

In the mid-1980s, anticipating a boom in tourism spurred by the 1984 Louisiana World Exposition, better known as the World's Fair, the Sheraton New Orleans Hotel opened across Canal Street from the Marriott. At forty-seven stories tall, the Sheraton is the tallest hotel in New Orleans and with its neighbors has changed the skyline of mostly low-level Canal Street forever. Also opening on the street around the same time was the Le Meridien, today a J. W. Marriott.

Many a high school prom was held at the Jung Hotel. (Photo by Del Hall)

The Marriott Hotel as seen from the top of the International Trade Mart (the World Trade Center) soon after the hotel opened in the early 1970s. (Courtesy of the family of G. E. Arnold and The Historic New Orleans Collection)

By the 1990s construction of new hotels had slowed considerably on Canal Street, but hotels were still being built as adaptive reuse of old buildings that would otherwise remain vacant. When Dillard's Department Stores took over the venerable old D. H. Holmes store in 1989, the building was donated to the city, which then leased it to a corporation that redeveloped it into the Chateau Sonesta Hotel. About a decade later the Maison Blanche Department Store and S. H. Kress variety store buildings were redeveloped as the luxurious Ritz-Carlton Hotel.

The twenty-first century has brought even more hotel conversions to Canal Street. The site of Marks Isaacs Department Store is now part of the Astor Crown Plaza. The other part of the hotel is in a new building with a facade designed as an interpretation of the 1890s store building that was torn down to build a Woolworth's store in the late 1940s.

With the emergence of so many hotels on Canal Street, depending on the time of year and which conventions are in town, the foot traffic at night creates a sought-after energy on this Great Wide Way—a reminder that the thoroughfare continues to maintain its place as New Orleans' main street.

Formerly D. H. Holmes Department Store, this structure was converted to the Chateau Sonesta Hotel in the 1990s.

The Hotel Astor Crown Plaza at the corner of Bourbon Street is on the site of part of a series of structures that comprised the commercial Touro Buildings. (Copyright 2002 by Robert S. Brantley)

CANAL STREET BY NIGHT, NEW ORLEANS, LA.

A postcard from about 1910 showing brilliantly lighted Canal Street at night.

CHAPTER FIVE
Signs from Above

CANAL STREET IS the Great Wide Way, and it was also the Great Bright Way. It was first illuminated at night by whale oil lamps, introduced to the city in the 1790s. Gaslight illuminated the street by 1832, and in the 1850s the thoroughfare was lined with ornate cast-iron light standards. The illumination it became known for was made possible in 1883 with the introduction of electric arc street lights. New Orleans was one of the first cities in the country to experiment with such lighting, matching the success of London, Paris, and New York, all far larger cities.

The first use of street arc lights in New Orleans was along the wharves, and the electric lines crossed the foot of Canal Street. Within a few months the popularity of this effort was apparent. By the mid-1880s, Canal Street was illuminated electrically all the way to the cemeteries. Half the distance was through near-open farm land. Although electricity was not common for home use until the 1920s, many businesses were connected to electric lines early on. This was despite the initial lack of insulation on wires. In wet weather, wires sparked, and if touched could cause electrocution.

The use of electricity came quickly to some Canal Street stores. By 1885 D. H. Holmes had shut off its gasoliers in favor of electric lights as lines were strung along its ceiling. When Maison Blanche opened in 1897, its mirror-lined show windows were lighted by hundreds of bare light bulbs, producing for over 100 feet along Canal Street a blaze of light unknown in most areas of town. Electric bulbs were strung along the facades of buildings and down either side of the neutral ground during Mardi Gras and Christmas.

People literally mobbed the street to see which of the clubs or dry goods stores could outdo the other and to enjoy the visual impact of the display. Like lavish window displays, electric light shows became "tradition" on Canal Street.

Initially, electric street lamps were tall wooden poles topped by light globes that constantly had to be replaced, since arc lights quickly burned out. Lights were also affixed to tall, wooden utility poles that supported a multitude of telegraph, telephone, and the ever-increasing electric wires needed to serve the expanding business district. The wires were so thickly strung in places that they not only threatened to topple but sometimes hindered firefighting efforts.

In an effort to concentrate and better support the wires, as well as to

"Canal Street, one of the widest streets in the United States, and reputed to be one of the best lighted streets in the world, is the center from which all activities in New Orleans radiate and the goal to which all return."

—*WPA New Orleans City Guide (1938)*

Many large towers such as this were built around New Orleans about 1887. They were meant to support the many utility wires and high-powered electric streetlights. They were torn down about 1899. (Courtesy of The Historic New Orleans Collection)

"improve" the lighting, a series of tall, iron derrick-like structures was erected around the center of the city about 1887. The tallest of these, almost 150 feet high, was in the center of Canal Street where Bourbon and Carondelet streets meet. It was a dismal failure, especially for lighting, since the single large arc lamp at the top did not evenly distribute the light, leaving eerie shadows under galleries and around corners.

In 1899, as bits and pieces of iron and wood were falling off the tower, Canal Street went through an extensive street beautification, and the tower was finally dismantled. The improvements included limiting the number of utility lines on poles along the median. New light standards were installed along the sidewalk and on the neutral ground. By this time Canal Street was one of the most brilliantly illuminated boulevards in the United States, and was depicted as such on postcards and in souvenir books. New Orleans had become a nighttime city.

In 1929 and 1930, Canal Street was completely repaved, and new streetcar tracks were laid. New light standards, which are still in use, were erected. They were ceremonially "lit" by Thomas Alva Edison from the post office in Fort Myers, Florida, on February 24, 1930, in a special program that attracted to Canal Street what was referred to as a "monster crowd" of people to witness the momentous event.

Lighting has long been an important form of signage along Canal Street. As soon as businesses began to invade the street, painted signs appeared on building facades advertising the emporiums inside. Soon buildings were almost covered with advertising lettering. At first, this was hardly visible after dark, since street lighting was so limited, but with the advent of gas lighting, illuminated signs and windows further brightened the nighttime darkness.

The Varieties Theater in the early 1870s had an arch of gaslights over its front entrance. With electricity came more brilliant displays. Along the street were signs that advertised hotels, theaters, and restaurants. The Grunewald Hotel, now the Fairmont, half a block off Canal, had its name spelled out in electric lights atop its roof, and D. H. Holmes electrically displayed its name along its Canal Street roof line.

The glare of light bulbs truly made Canal Street not only a Great Wide Way, but also a Great White Way. In the 1920s Canal Street became more colorful with the advent of neon gas lighting, developed in France in 1911. Neon lights consisted of glass tubes containing neon gas that glowed red or blue when electricity was passed through them. Soon flourescent powders made it possible to produce other colors, and designers in the 1930s began to experiment with lighting ideas as static neon lighting gave way to animated billboards rising high above buildings.

Canal Street became a Great Bright Way of signs and billboards by the late 1930s as neon creations flashed along its business blocks. Over 80 percent of the signs on Canal Street were neon, and that figure held for thirty years. Indeed, Canal Street's great width was ideal for such signage. The visual impact would have been less in a narrower setting. Many stores had colorful, lighted name signs, such as the vertical blue sign

A night view during the early 1960s shows many commercial signs on Canal Street. A pastime for locals was to go downtown to window shop and look at the signs sparkling with neon and colored bulbs. (Photo by Dorothy Violet Gulledge; courtesy of the New Orleans Public Library)

A neon sign welcoming Sugar Bowl visitors was part of the colorful Canal Street skyline during the early 1960s. (Photo by Dorothy Violet Gulledge; courtesy of the New Orleans Public Library)

Looking toward the Mississippi River, one can see signs for the Tudor Theatre and the locally brewed Regal Beer among the many that decorated the Canal Street skyline. (Photo by Dorothy Violet Gulledge; courtesy of the New Orleans Public Library)

For many years, atop the Joy Theatre was a brilliant neon sign advertising Canadian
Club whiskey. It was replaced in the 1990s by a sign for the Powerball lottery game.
(Photo courtesy of Rene Brunet)

identifying Holmes. Still extant are the neon lights on Walgreens drug store. Even more noticeable were the big advertising signs high above roof lines for products such as Calvert and Canadian Club whiskeys and Falstaff and Jax beer.

Edmond M. Brignac, Sr. of Industrial Electric, Inc. was responsible for much of the street's more creative signage. There was an animated cartoon for Karno the Tailor, and a huge neon clock and advertising sign could be seen at the Coca-Cola plant near the Canal Street ferry ramp. A tri-fold sign for National Food Stores was made up of a series of simultaneously turning facets revealing three different images and a Times Square-type message sign around the bottom.

Modern plastic signage and zoning ordinances have limited the size and intrusion of lighted billboards. This has altered the often flashing, colorful lights that helped give Canal Street its bright and eye-catching allure. And while Canal Street is still wide and bright at night, the Great Wide Way is today somewhat more subdued.

Protecting shoppers from the light of day in the summer months or the rain just about any time of the year were ornate cast-iron galleries. The Touro Block was ringed with them. By 1850 this fashion had taken New Orleans by storm, and they were not only being included on many new buildings, but were being added to old ones as well. Cast iron prevailed along the main shopping portion of Canal Street, and was

Detail of the Canadian Club whiskey sign.

Industrial Electric Company's Edmond Brignac, Sr. was responsible for many of Canal Street's more creative signage. This sign, for Karno's men's clothing store, featured an animated stick figure in its advertisement. (Courtesy of Rene Brunet)

Even at night, Canal Street was and still is a busy place. This photo was taken in the early 1960s. (Photo courtesy of Del Hall)

For the duration of World War II, a huge American flag was draped down the front of the Godchaux's store. Its popularity was such that a postcard was made of the view. (Courtesy of The Historic New Orleans Collection)

Sears and Roebuck, a block away from Canal Street in the curve of Baronne Street, always used its highly visible location to best advantage, such as during World War II when a billboard was erected promoting the purchase of war bonds. (Courtesy of The Historic New Orleans Collection)

A 1941 example of Canal Street as the Great Bright Way. (Photo by Gene Leingang; courtesy of Bergeron Gallery)

fashionable and attractive. Until the early twentieth century, lacy iron-work galleries and balconies were as much a part of Canal Street as they were in the French Quarter.

By the end of the nineteenth century, such embellishments were going out of fashion, and even considered provincial looking when compared to the architecture of other large cities. Ironwork was slowly pulled off buildings along Canal Street. Finally, in 1930, the last remaining iron-work was ordered removed by city ordinance as part of a street beautifi-cation project. In a return to the past, some contemporary buildings, including the Astor Crown Plaza Hotel, have included cast iron in their designs, giving a glimpse of what late nineteenth-century Canal Street looked like.

Banners signifying special events have added to the allure of Canal Street. Banners welcoming pioneer aviator Charles Lindbergh to New Orleans in 1927, signs commemorating the Eucharistic Congress, an international meeting of Catholics in 1938, and a sign atop Sears and Roebuck urging the purchase of World War II war bonds all illustrate how the thoroughfare has served as a "bulletin board."

Bright and usually colorful neon illuminated Canal Street's night sky beginning in the 1920s. One of the most eye-catching was the sign at the Coca-Cola Bottling Plant, seen here in 1952, next to the Algiers ferry ramp. (Courtesy of The Historic New Orleans Collection)

In 1977, when the New Orleans Museum of Art hosted the Treasures of Tutankamen, D. H. Holmes welcomed the event with a giant banner of old King Tut himself that hung above the store's front entrance. Looking out across the street at Canal Street's jewelry stores, the pharaoh, known for his penchant for baubles, should have felt right at home.

Canal Street is decorated here in October 1927 for the visit of Charles Lindbergh after his solo flight across the Atlantic Ocean to Paris. Except for a few changes, Canal Street from this vantage point near St. Charles remains much the same. (Courtesy of The Historic New Orleans Collection)

CHAPTER SIX

As Meeting Place

THE MOST AUSPICIOUS gathering place on late-Victorian Canal Street was the Henry Clay Monument, where Royal and St. Charles streets meet. Although Clay was not from Louisiana, he had many personal and professional connections to the state, and was regarded as one of its sons. He was considered one of the nation's great statesmen, especially after having prevented an earlier civil war, causing him to be nicknamed "the Great Pacificator."

Upon his death in 1852, plans were set in motion to erect a monument in his honor in New Orleans. The cornerstone was laid in 1856, and in 1860 a bronze figure of Clay by Joel T. Hart was unveiled atop a granite shaft set on an octagonal base with gas lights. At the dedication, there was a three-mile-long procession, and dense crowds of people congregated along Canal Street.

The monument soon became a traffic hazard as streetcar lines were installed in ever-increasing numbers along Canal Street. City officials often called for the removal of the monument, but there was always stiff public resistance to protect what was considered by many people to have sentimental value. People met friends there—as they did under the clock at Holmes in later days—and they gathered there on Mardi Gras or for events such as the annual firemen's parade. Indeed, virtually every important New Orleans parade passed the monument.

In 1895 the railing and

The Henry Clay Monument as seen from Exchange Place about 1882. Stone street paving and the street's deep gutters are clearly visible. In the distance is one of the city's first electric streetlights. (Courtesy of The Historic New Orleans Collection)

Election-day crowds around 1873 on Canal Street between St. Charles and Carondelet. This was the heart of the shopping district at the time, and Moreau's was among the best restaurants in the city. (Courtesy of The Historic New Orleans Collection)

steps of the Henry Clay Monument were removed and the ornate base reduced to ease the realignment of new tracks and wires for electric streetcars. Finally, in January 1901, the monument was moved to the center of Lafayette Square where it still stands. There was public grumbling about the removal, and some proposals were advanced to keep the monument on Canal Street. One idea was to build a large, table-like base on which the monument would be lifted, allowing space for the streetcars to pass unhindered below it.

One event that was popular in the late nineteenth and early twentieth centuries was Straw Hat Day. This was at a time when men were still expected to wear hats as part of their seasonal wardrobe. During the summer, straw boaters and panamas were worn by practically every man.

Straw Hat Day was the first Sunday in October and signaled the end of another summer in New Orleans. Men took their faded and worn straw hats to a cannon at the foot of Canal Street. The hats were then stuffed into the cannon and shot across the Mississippi River to mark the end of another hot, humid, and then un-air conditioned summer.

Canal Street at Monkey Wrench Corner, where Royal and St. Charles meet, about 1884. The tall roof on the left belonged to the then-new Pickwick Club at the corner of Carondelet Street. (Courtesy of The Historic New Orleans Collection)

On a summer day in 1928, women wear white dresses and cloche hats and men sport suits and straw hats. This dressy clothing was typical Canal Street attire at the time. (Courtesy of The Historic New Orleans Collection)

Newspaper advertisements for men's stores of the day advised that their customers should get rid of their straw hats at the foot of Canal Street and replace them with new ones for the upcoming fall and winter season.

For many years Canal Street was the heart of "Club Land," important private meeting places. Although the Boston Club has been in its current location on Canal Street since 1884, many clubs rarely stayed put. For instance, the Pickwick Club was founded in 1857 and has had ten homes, of which seven have been on Canal Street. In 1884 the club moved into a formidable Queen Anne-style building at the corner of Carondelet Street. Ten years later it vacated the facility when a fire razed the roof. The building later housed Fellman's and Feibleman's dry good stores. It was demolished in the late 1940s and replaced by the Gus Mayer store.

In 1896 the Pickwick Club relocated to 1028 Canal Street, but left that building, which is still in commercial use, in 1934. Since 1950 the Pickwick Club has been housed in an historic building at the corner of St. Charles. Constructed in 1821, it originally housed the Crescent City Billiards Hall. The structure was essentially rebuilt in 1875, and except for storefront alterations on the ground floor, is still standing. The ground floor was the site of a Russell Stover candy store for many years.

In 1883 the Chess, Checkers, and Whist Club moved into the Perry House Hotel at the corner of Baronne Street. After the building burned, a new structure with a distinctive corner cupola was built on the same site. The club continued to meet there until 1920. The building was torn

The Chess, Checkers, and Whist Club is seen here in 1895 at the corner of Baronne Street. The Grunewald Hotel is in the background. (Courtesy of The Historic New Orleans Collection)

down in the late 1930s, and a Walgreens drug store has occupied the site ever since.

Orleanians have always gravitated to Canal Street, whether in protest or celebration—or just to pull the community together. During World War I, several Liberty Bond parades brought out crowds of spectators, as did visiting fundraisers such as Charlie Chaplin and Mary Pickford.

In October 1918, just weeks before Armistice Day, hundreds of thousands of people poured onto Canal Street. This was against the advice of local doctors who were warning that the "sneeze plague," better known as Spanish influenza, was on the verge of striking the city. Patriotism ruled, but only after thousands fell ill in one of the worst epidemics ever to strike New Orleans. Flu or not, when the Armistice was signed on November 11, 1918, New Orleanians again flooded the street to celebrate. Trucks and cars paraded down the street in a delirium of joy to celebrate the end of the "war to end all wars."

After the United States entered World War I in 1917, war bond sales took place across the nation. Virtually all were accompanied by large parades such as this one on Canal Street. (Courtesy of The Historic New Orleans Collection)

Sarah Bernhardt was one of the celebrities who came to New Orleans in 1918 as part of a national tour to sell war bonds during World War I. (Courtesy of The Historic New Orleans Collection)

This was one of twenty temporary monuments put up along Canal Street in 1918 to honor the men killed during World War I. (Courtesy of The Historic New Orleans Collection)

An exciting time for all the city's residents, not just its Roman Catholics, was the Eighth National Eucharistic Congress October 17-20, 1938. This was a huge gathering, with roots in the 1880s, to honor ancient devotion to the Holy Sacrament. Large numbers of delegates came to New Orleans from across the nation. Altars were specially decorated across town, and stores along Canal Street welcomed the many visitors. A parade of thousands of people passed along the length of Canal Street, and the Eucharistic Congress culminated in a great open air Mass held in City Park Stadium.

In 1939 Europe was at war again, and a little over two years later, after

During World War I, celebrities such as Charlie Chaplin, shown on a visit to New Orleans, traveled across the United States promoting the sale of war bonds. (Courtesy of The Historic New Orleans Collection)

A large war bond campaign in 1918 was accompanied by a parade on Canal Street. (Courtesy of The Historic New Orleans Collection)

During the war bond parade in 1918, Mardi Gras float designers Soulié and Crassons assembled several floats that resembled tanks. *(Courtesy of The Historic New Orleans Collection)*

During the Eucharistic Congress in 1938, a large public Mass was held in City Park, along with a parade on Canal Street, seen here in a photograph by Charles L. Franck Photographers. The procession passes Warren Easton High School, in the background. *(Courtesy of The Historic New Orleans Collection)*

In 1938 New Orleans, a city with a strong Catholic heritage, was chosen to host the Eucharistic Congress of the Roman Catholic Church. In recognition of the event, many stores along Canal Street, including D. H. Holmes, shown here, displayed appropriate decorations. (Courtesy of the Archives of the Archdiocese of New Orleans)

the Japanese attack on Pearl Harbor, the United States declared war as well. On Canal Street Godchaux's displayed a seven-story American flag that covered most of the store. Colorful advertising posters drawn by Works Progress Administration artists appeared along the thoroughfare urging Americans to buy war bonds, not to divulge information to the enemy, to conserve food, and to watch out for venereal disease.

V-E Day—Victory in Europe—in May 1945 again brought crowds into Canal Street. But even greater numbers hit the street a few months later in a great celebration of V-J Day—Victory over Japan—since that marked the end of World War II. Within minutes after the Japanese surrender was announced, houses of worship filled with thankful people. Others took to the streets to celebrate.

For many New Orleanians, the euphoria and spontaneity of these victory celebrations made the pleasure of Mardi Gras pale in comparison. But everybody knew that the end of the war meant that Carnival celebrations—cancelled for the duration of the conflict—would soon return.

*The Henry Clay Monument was the gathering place for the White League when it bat-
tled the metropolitan police in 1874. (Courtesy of The Historic New Orleans Collection)*

CHAPTER SEVEN
Social Issues

As New Orleans' great gathering place, Canal Street has at times been the site of demonstrations, some of them angry. Some landmarks have even become symbolic of the dispute.

One example is the Liberty Monument, which was erected in 1891 on the Canal Street neutral ground between today's Saks Fifth Avenue and Harrah's Casino. It commemorates the Battle of September 14, 1874. The confrontation in front of the Custom House pitted a group of white businessmen called the White League against the mostly black metropolitan police. It was one of the major conflicts of the Reconstruction era, and southern whites of the time considered it a victory for states rights. To others, it was worthy only of condemnation.

The Liberty Monument, which honors the fallen members of the White League, consists of a granite obelisk supported by four Corinthian columns. It had been part of a display in the World's Industrial and Cotton Centennial Exposition held in Audubon Park in 1884-85. Over the years, several inscriptions proclaiming white supremacy were added to the memorial, providing further controversy.

The monument was put in storage for some time, and has been threatened with dismantlement. Protected as an historic site, it has been moved to Wells Street, about a block off Canal Street. It is hidden between an electrical power facility and the parking garage of Canal Place and is missing one of its support columns.

The Henry Clay Monument was the rallying point for the White League in 1874. It was used again as an assembly point for a protest on March 14, 1891. The latter was in response to the acquittal of a number of Italians who had been accused of killing the New Orleans Chief of Police David Hennessey the previous year. A mob marched from Canal Street to Orleans Parish Prison, located then on Orleans Avenue (near today's Morris F. X. Jeff Municipal Auditorium). The group broke into the grim, dilapidated old building and shot the Italian suspects and hanged two others. Outrage reverberated throughout the country and in Italy.

Most whites retained pleasant memories of Canal Street as it existed prior to the mid-1960s, but many in the black community did not. In the days of racial segregation prior to the passage of the 1964 Civil Rights Act, black New Orleanians were able to shop on Canal Street, but not all stores allowed them to try on clothing.

SOCIAL ISSUES ON CANAL STREET

"You kind of knew as you grew up where you had to go. You had a mental map because if you were in the wrong place and you needed to use the restroom or needed a drink of water, you couldn't use it." The days of racial segregation are gone but not forgotten by University of New Orleans history professor Dr. Raphael Cassimere and many other black people who shopped on Canal Street up until the mid-1960s.

Cassimere was president of the National Association for the Advancement of Colored People Youth Council from 1960 to 1966. "1963 was the pivotal year in the Civil Rights movement," recalls Cassimere. "Along with other black activist organizations such as the Congress of Racial Equality (CORE), this was when we began what became a two-year boycott of over thirty-five stores to get people hired at other than a menial level and desegregate public facilities. We thought it was going to be quick and easy, that we were going to be out in two or three weeks, and it lasted for over two years."

Retired Xavier University

During the early 1960s, members of the National Association for the Advancement of Colored People (NAACP) Youth Council and other organizations picketed Canal Street merchants seeking increased minority employment and better treatment. (Courtesy of Dr. Raphael Cassimere, Jr. and the Louisiana and Special Collections Departments/Earl K. Long Library, University of New Orleans)

administrator Sybil Morial, the widow of former New Orleans Mayor Ernest "Dutch" Morial, vividly recalls the Canal Street boycotts. "For a long, long time I didn't put my foot in any of those stores. Some of the malls were open then. I went to Gentilly Woods and that's where we shopped. We reduced our buying because it was a very tense time. It was only when they began to hire black salespersons that we felt, well, we're a part of this now."

The Liberty Place Monument was erected in the 1890s on the Canal Street neutral ground near the Mississippi riverfront to commemorate the victory of the White League over the mostly black metropolitan police. Now considered to be politically incorrect by some, the historic landmark has been moved to a less prominent spot a block off Canal Street.

Water fountains were segregated and presented at times a now-odd configuration of two high fountains—one each for black and white adults—and two lower fountains for children of each race. Blacks could not eat at department store restaurants, cafes, or some lunch counters along Canal Street, and it was at the lunch counters at stores such as Woolworth's that civil rights activists held sit-ins in acts of public disobedience. Boycotts and civil rights marches were staged on Canal Street.

One result of segregation was that blacks were less likely to shop on Canal Street than to patronize stores on South Rampart Street. Some national chain stores, including Thom McAn Shoes and National Shirt Shops, had stores on South Rampart Street as well as Canal Street.

In the early 1950s, a shoe store on South Rampart Street held a grand opening sale. To promote the sale, it employed two attractive young women dressed in skimpy pirate costumes. One of the women was white, the other was black. The long line of men waiting to get into the store included both races, underscoring the more tolerant attitudes toward shopping on South Rampart Street in pre-civil rights days.

As the city's new drainage system went into operation after 1900, low-lying areas, including the area that became known as Mid-City, grew quickly. New Orleans' pent-up need for expansion and new housing was being satisfied, and those families that could afford to do so exchanged old inner-city houses for newer ones elsewhere with modern design and amenities. Older neighborhoods in New Orleans tended to be racially mixed, but in the era of expanding segregation the new neighborhoods were not, nor were most of the new public schools. As whites left old neighborhoods, poor whites and blacks remained behind. A similar population shift occurred in the "white flight" of young families to suburbs being built outside the city limits a half-century later.

Today's Canal Street beyond the shopping district is far less residential than seventy-five years ago, with many of the larger homes being used as small businesses, such as law firms. Off Canal Street, the streets closer to downtown have a larger black population. Toward the end of the thoroughfare, the neighborhoods are now a mix of black and white residents.

"As children," says Cassimere, "we couldn't go certain places and were not always told why. You know, maybe the easy thing for parents was to invent some excuse why their children couldn't go places where they saw other children of different races going," he adds, "so it wasn't so much painful as puzzling. But as I grew older and became a little more aware of what was going on, then of course I wanted to try and change it."

"When I was growing up it was rigid segregation and we couldn't go to any of the restaurants," Morial continues. "There were lunch counters in the back of the stores, in Woolworth's, Grant's, and McCrory's. It was always a practice in our house that before we went shopping we had to be sure we had enough to eat. I think my mother tried to protect us from any insults or bad incidents."

"Integrating Canal Street was a broad-based endeavor," says Cassimere. "One thing that most people need to realize is that it was an effort made by a lot of people, young people, older people, blacks and whites, Jews and Gentiles, Catholics and Protestants. And while there was a lot of sacrifice involved, there was also this feeling that something positive was happening."

During the late nineteenth and early twentieth centuries, revelers converged on Canal Street on Christmas Eve to shop, shoot fireworks, and make noise. In 1884 one group of boys made this oversized horn. (Courtesy of The Historic New Orleans Collection)

CHAPTER EIGHT
The Christmas Season

RETAILING AND THE EVOLUTION of large show windows with bright lights helped bring about a popular pastime of window shopping, as merchants showed off their wares to greatest advantage. In the mid-nineteenth century, show windows were generally filled to overflowing with merchandise. Displays were presented with little sense of order, and some merchants tried to show examples of everything in stock.

As the century progressed, order came to show windows, since only selected goods were being displayed and seasonal embellishments made the windows a more attractive setting. In the early twentieth century, dressed mannequins began to appear in special settings. This gave the windows an extravagant and theatrical look that attracted window shoppers. Store windows along Canal Street became another form of entertainment.

This was especially true during the Christmas season, as department and fashion stores vied with each other to design the most eye-catching

The brightly lighted show windows of Maison Blanche on Christmas Eve 1899. (Courtesy of The Historic New Orleans Collection)

"JINGLE, JANGLE, JINGLE . . . HERE COMES MR. BINGLE"

Who would have thought that a snowman puppet sporting an ice cream cone hat would become one of a semi-tropical city's most beloved symbols of Christmas? Well, blame it on . . . actually, let's tip our hat to . . . the late Emile Alline, Sr., former display director for Maison Blanche Department Stores.

Mr. Bingle, a snowman marionette, was the mascot of Maison Blanche Department Store. A live show featuring Bingle and friends was held throughout the day in the front window of the Canal Street store during the Christmas season. (Courtesy of Jeff Kent)

On a 1947 trip to Chicago he noticed that other stores had adopted mascots. When he returned, Alline pitched to store officials, including Maison Blanche advertising director Lewis "Doonie" Schwarz, Jr., the concept of a snowman brought to life by Santa Claus. The rest is local history. Maison Blanche president Herbert Schwartz named the figure Mr. Bingle, a name incorporating the store's initials.

One theory as to the origin of the name comes from Ashleigh Austin, who has a portion of her own website (AshleighAustin.com) dedicated to Bingle lore. In addition to noting that the name Bingle has a holiday ring to it, "like Kris Kringle," she cites a 1915 novel by George Barr McCutcheon, a bestselling author of forty-two novels, including *Brewster's Millions.* In his novel called *Mr. Bingle,* McCutcheon writes of a childless couple, Mr. and Mrs. Thomas S. Bingle, who take less fortunate children into their modest New York apartment on Christmas Eve, fix dinner, and shower them with presents. Mr. Bingle reads Dickens' *A Christmas Carol* to them.

So, could McCutcheon's book have graced Mr. Schwartz's night table? Probably.

Bingle made his debut as Maison Blanche mascot during the Christmas season of 1948, and a giant papier-mâché version adorned the facade of the Canal Street store for half a century. Emile Alline, Sr. decided to mount a puppet show for the establishment's front windows.

D. H. Holmes Christmas decorations in the 1950s. (Photo by C. F. Weber; courtesy of Bergeron Gallery)

A must stop for Christmas shoppers was the front windows of D. H. Holmes Department Store. (Photo by C. F. Weber; courtesy of Bergeron Gallery)

A generous budget made for lavish Christmas displays in the front windows of D. H. Holmes Department Store, shown here in the late 1960s. (Photo by C. F. Weber; courtesy of Bergeron Gallery)

Winter wonderlands were often a part of the Christmas window display at D. H. Holmes.

Puppeteer Edwin "Oscar" Isentrout gave Maison Blanche's popular Mr. Bingle his sprite-like personality. (Courtesy of Jeff Kent)

Puppeteer Edwin H. "Oscar" Isentrout was hired by Maison Blanche executive Emile Alline, Sr. to create a snowman mascot for the department store. (Courtesy of Jeff Kent)

He hired a tall and lanky veteran puppeteer named Edwin H. "Oscar" Isentrout, who had been performing on Bourbon Street in a show that featured puppets doing a strip tease. Isentrout was given a workshop, and from it came Bingle, a family-friendly snow sprite. Assisting Isentrout during those formative days were puppeteers Harry J. Ory and Ray Frederick.

Puppeteer Jeff Kent worked with Isentrout as an apprentice. He recalls what Isentrout told him:

> At Christmas time, on Canal Street, they would create these wonderful window displays and they would have a show. There were two or three puppeteers up in the ceiling of the

window, called "the loft." And they would operate the marionettes from that loft. There was a prerecorded soundtrack, and speakers were mounted outside the windows on Canal Street at Maison Blanche. The shows would last ten to fifteen minutes. Mr. Bingle would come out and say, "Please make sure that you leave enough room for the little ones to enjoy the show." Because there'd be groups of people that were like ten, fifteen deep. Hundreds of people would come. And it used to drive the police crazy because during Christmas time, when they did the shows, there'd be so many people just outside the building watching the show that you would have to go out into the street to walk around the crowd. Because the crowd was that deep. It would go all the way to the curb.

Oscar Isentrout even gave Bingle a voice, which came in handy for a short television show that was broadcast on WDSU-TV in the 1950s and into the 1970s. Bingle's voice was squeaky and high-pitched.

"He was a dear, and you know he really was Mr. Bingle," recalls New Orleans entertainment critic Al Shea, who played Bingle's pal "Pete the Penguin" in the fifteen-minute television program that

During the 1950s Mr. Bingle had his own television show on WDSU-TV. (Courtesy of Jeff Kent)

After D. H. Holmes was remodeled in 1965, a display of bells was hung across the store's front each Christmas season. The bells swung as though tolling in synchronization with Christmas music. (From the Vieux Carre Survey; courtesy of The Historic New Orleans Collection)

and elaborate displays. Beginning about the 1850s, seasonal greens, religious paintings, and even lighted candles appeared in holiday windows alongside the shopkeeper's most expensive merchandise. As the twentieth century progressed, holiday windows became more elaborate. Luxury stores, including Gus Mayer, Godchaux's, Kreeger's, and Goldring's, showed wonderlands of furs, designer evening dresses, expensive lingerie, cosmetics, and fragrances in Christmas-card settings.

For late nineteenth century New Orleanians, one of the great annual gatherings along Canal Street aside from Mardi Gras was on Christmas Eve. While many families spent that evening in church and in quiet family gatherings, there were thousands of others who streamed to Canal Street to gaze at the decorated show windows. At that time the holiday season began not the day after Thanksgiving but on Christmas Eve, and most stores stayed open until after midnight. The sight of street vendors lining the thoroughfare hawking their goods resembled a street festival.

For some people, that meant dressing up—many people actually came from church—and to see and be seen. For others, especially youngsters, it meant blowing horns, beating drums, and shooting fireworks. Today, the use of fireworks has shifted from Christmas Eve to New Year's Eve. Back then, even the shooting of firearms was regarded as normal. There were always shooting injuries on Christmas Eve, and Christmas Day

The Christmas Season ❖ 123

At its high-profile location a block from Canal Street in the bend of Baronne Street, Sears and Roebuck annually installed a large cutout Santa Claus figure.

For post-World War II Baby Boomers in New Orleans, the snowman Mr. Bingle at Maison Blanche was as much a symbol of the Christmas season as Santa Claus himself, shown here about 1950 in a photograph by Charles L. Franck Photographers. (Courtesy of The Historic New Orleans Collection)

aired weekday afternoons before Christmas. "He moved up an octave but not much. And the kids loved him. He was very charity minded. He did all the hospitals, all the schools, all free."

So what made this little snowman figure so cute?

"Mr. Bingle is a child," says Kent. "He is a child that likes to have fun. He gets into mischief. If you listen to some of the old recordings of the Mr. Bingle window shows, it's usually Mr. Bingle who gets into trouble, And Santa Claus usually gets him out of trouble."

Isentrout died in 1985 but the spry little snowman, not unlike those fabled sugar plums, continues to dance around in the heads of Baby Boomers whose parents shopped at Maison Blanche. Dillard's Department Store chain, which purchased Maison Blanche, offers a line of Bingle merchandise, and while the puppet show is no more, snipping those strings of memory is just about impossible.

A unicorn was one of many mythical figures in the intricate displays in the front windows at D. H. Holmes. (Photo by C. F. Weber, courtesy of Bergeron Gallery)

THE CENTANNI HOUSE

One Canal Street resident's love for her children and Christmas resulted in some indelibly etched memories for many Orleanians.

For two decades, Myra Collins Centanni, with the help of her husband, Salvador ("Sam") Centanni, and their seven children, decorated the yard at their Art Nouveau-inspired home that sits atop terraced land at 4506 Canal Street and South Murat Street. The family business, the nearby Gold Seal Creamery, was a Mid-City fixture and known for its Creole cream cheese.

From 1946 until 1966, the family added to Santa's workshop a life-size Nativity scene and

The porch of the Centanni house, brilliantly illuminated for Christmas. (Courtesy of the family of Myra Centanni Mehrtens)

Santa Claus at the Centanni house. Note the rocket ship. (Courtesy of the family of Myra Centanni Mehrtens)

A portrait of the Madonna was on view as part of the D. H. Holmes Christmas decorations in the late 1960s. (Photo by C. F. Weber; courtesy of Bergeron Gallery)

newspapers give the impression that such accidents were just to be expected. The noise of fireworks, tin drums, and screaming tin horns usually reached a maddening tumult, and it could last for days.

The Christmas Eve gathering on Canal Street began around the 1840s, and as the street grew in importance, much of the activity gravitated to that street as the nineteenth century wore on. This was especially the case after the introduction of electric lights and shop owners began to string their buildings with displays of lights. After 1900 the Christmas Eve gatherings on Canal Street began to decline, and they ended around World War I. This was partly because of the earlier start of the Christmas season, having been moved closer to Thanksgiving. Christmas Eve was spent more and more at home or with family, and street activities were moved to New Year's Eve.

By the twentieth century, department stores, with their extra window space, were able to present spectacular holiday displays. Beginning in the mid-1960s, D. H. Holmes annually graced the front of its store with a carillon of bells synchronized with recorded yuletide music. With some of the city's most lavish displays of Christmas windows, Holmes regularly included animated figures in a wonderland of light and color. One year there might be eighteenth-century figures in the French court, while in another Victorian figures were shown celebrating the holiday season. Yet another showed monkeys dressed in eighteenth-century finery who

Parades were long a part of the Christmas season on Canal Street. This is a float from a parade in the 1930s. (Courtesy of the New Orleans Public Library)

The entire exterior of the Centanni house was decorated, including the side yards and porches. (Courtesy of the family of Myra Centanni Mehrtens)

Colorful Christmas decorations on the porch of the Centanni House during the daytime. Note the elephant. (Courtesy of the family of Myra Centanni Mehrtens)

progressively tore the outfits off each other.

One of the last holiday seasons at Holmes saw windows filled with frolicking teddy bears. The windows were not revealed as a rule until the day after Thanksgiving. For many years, in addition to having children sit on his lap for photos, the Santa at D. H. Holmes also waved to passersby from the balcony above the Canal Street entrance way.

During one Christmas season before it closed in the 1960s, Marks Isaacs set up a window of little animated circus figures. Although not on Canal Street, the four-story Santa Claus on the front of Sears and Roebuck on Baronne at Common streets could be easily seen from Canal Street.

It was left to Maison Blanche to give New Orleans its most loveable Christmas icon in the character of Mr. Bingle, a cheery snowman with a hat made from an ice cream cone. Bingle was created in 1948 by Maison Blanche window decorator Emile Alline, Sr. and given a personality by puppeteer Edwin H. "Oscar" Isentrout. Mr. Bingle had not only his own show window with a wintry wonderland setting and a stage on which to perform for the kids and Santa, but the little snowman also performed on his own television program during the season to help kids decide what to request from Santa. A giant figure of Mr. Bingle also extended across several stories of the tall Maison Blanche facade.

Rudolph, complete with the other reindeer. Also on view for a few years was an unexpected elephant. In an interview with the New Orleans *Times Picayune* in the 1980s, Myra Centanni Mehrtens, one of Myra and Sam's daughters, recalled that her mom had read to her family that year a children's book that had a circus theme. Forget the big top, there's an elephant on the lawn!

A youngster from Chalmette drew inspiration from what he and his family saw when they visited the home. Amid the hubbub of cotton-candy salesmen, traffic congestion, and crowds of onlookers, Popeye's Fried Chicken founder Al Copeland decided that he would decorate his own home

Central to the Centanni home Christmas decorations was a Nativity scene. It was donated to City Park and is part of its Celebration in the Oaks display. (Courtesy of the family of Myra Centanni Mehrtens)

for Christmas when he grew up. In his 2003 display at his home on Folse Drive in Metairie, he included a replica of the Centanni home.

Tragically, the annual decorating efforts stopped in 1966 when Mrs. Centanni died of a heart attack on New Year's Day in the arms of her husband while they were dancing at a birthday party in his honor in their basement party room.

The figures from the Nativity scene have been preserved and are on view at City Park's Celebration in the Oaks display.

But, of course, it wasn't only the decorations that drew attention to this house. It was the design of the structure itself. Built in 1915 for paving contractor William H. Kane, the home was designed by architect H. Jordan McKenzie, whose own home on West End Boulevard in Lakeview sported a blue ceramic tile roof.

After Kane died, other owners included W. H. Crowley and Dr. Virgil Jackson, who sold it to the Centannis in 1944.

According to architectural historian Robert Cangelosi, McKenzie

A French Quarter scene of a student with a nun shows the detail that was part of the D. H. Holmes Christmas window displays. (Photo by Dorothy Violet Gulledge; courtesy of the New Orleans Public Library)

Thanks to Betty Finnin, the City of New Orleans' official city decorator, the light standards on the Canal Street neutral ground were decked out for holidays, especially Christmas. She served from 1933 until 1970, when the position was not funded in the city budget. Candy canes, figures from children's stories, actual trees, and traditional Christmas wreaths were among the decorations that graced the street's lamp posts.

Another "must" stop downtown was the lobby of the Roosevelt Hotel (now the Fairmont). During the Christmas season there was a tunnel of cotton-like batting decorated with Christmas bells and ornaments. Discontinued for many years due to the flammability of the materials, the tradition returned to the hotel in the 1990s. Also decked out for the season with Christmas trees in its lobby was the St. Charles Hotel. Known in its final days as the Sheraton-Charles, it was demolished in the 1970s.

In a city of parades, it is not surprising that Christmas processions

During the Christmas season, Mr. Bingle, with his wings of holly, was a familiar sight above the entrance of Maison Blanche on Canal Street. (Photo by David Richmond)

The tall light standards erected in 1929-30 have always lent themselves well to decorating during the Christmas and Carnival seasons. (Courtesy of the New Orleans Public Library)

The snowfall of New Year's Eve in 1963 in New Orleans covers a reindeer and other decorations at the Centanni home. (Courtesy of the family of Myra Centanni Mehrtens)

was influenced by the work of Austrian architect Josef Maria Olbrich. McKenzie saw the German Pavilion that Olbrich had designed for the 1904 St. Louis Fair. The Art Noveau style celebrated individual craftsmanship and used the newer forms and materials that had become available.

The front of the home is anchored by a staircase that leads to an enormous porch. What cannot be missed is the prominent almost "winged" roof. This bungalow house was dubbed a "House of Tomorrow" for an Electric Association of New Orleans promotional campaign and featured an elevator, intercom, and marble steam bath. The home was sold by the Centanni family in 2003 and is being restored.

Canal Street had a lot of "eye candy" during the Christmas season, such as these candy canes on a light standard near the Loew's State Theatre. The display was created with the help of decorator Betty Finnin. (Courtesy of the New Orleans Public Library)

Christmas decorations adorn Canal Street's light standards as the massive Roosevelt (now Fairmont) Hotel looms over the street.

Even though Mr. Bingle was the star at Maison Blanche during the 1950s, this Santa held the attention of many a youngster. (Courtesy of Peggy Scott Laborde)

New Orleans actress Adella Gautier with Santa and nephew Roy Meyers. Prior to the Civil Rights Act, black children could not visit Santa Claus at most big Canal Street department stores. After the legislation was passed, stores made it a point to welcome every child. (Courtesy of Adella Gautier)

In 1957 flocked Christmas trees were part of the decor of the Sheraton Charles Hotel lobby. (Photo by Leon Trice; courtesy of Special Collections/Tulane University)

The Krewe of Proteus parade in 2002. The Mardi Gras organization dates back to 1882 and is one of only two organizations from the nineteenth century that still parades. (Courtesy of Peggy Scott Laborde)

Canal Street's Texaco Building decorated for the Christmas season. (Courtesy of The Historic New Orleans Collection)

have been held on Canal Street throughout the years to usher in the season. Aside from Christmas time, many special events brought customers to Canal Street. Sales were not then the almost daily events of today, but were held only at certain times. Twice a year Community Bargain Days were held by virtually every store in town. Some of the best merchandise was offered at the best prices. There were even bus coupons that could be cut out of the newspaper for a free ride to Canal Street.

Special international events were also regularly held each year, at a time when international travel was not as common as today. These international events were sponsored by the big stores that sold special imports. Displays and demonstrations provided extra excitement to the shopping scene, and store restaurants offered foreign-inspired fare. For a week or two the goods and flags of the world decorated Canal Street.

On December 31, 1963, Canal Street became a winter wonderland and its Christmas decorations were covered with snow in one of the heaviest snowfalls in the city's history. (Photo courtesy of the family of G. E. Arnold and The Historic New Orleans Collection)

Mr. Bingle, on the Canal Street entrance overhang at left, reminds shoppers 'tis the season. (Photo by Del Hall)

Among the most lavish and popular displays at Christmas was the 300-foot-long lobby of the Roosevelt (today Fairmont) Hotel where the walls and ceiling were flocked to resemble a winter wonderland in semi-tropical New Orleans. This scene is from the 1960s. The tradition was discontinued for a time but returned in the 1990s. (Courtesy of the Fairmont Hotel)

CHAPTER NINE
Mardi Gras

WHILE SOME EUROPEAN cities are able to claim that they have streets frequently traveled by kings and queens, in the United States there is one place that can make the same assertion. Canal Street during the Carnival season has long been America's street of kings, with many different monarchs reigning from year to year.

Though Mardi Gras has been celebrated in New Orleans from its earliest days, the festival as New Orleanians have come to know it dates to 1857 with the first parade of the Mistick Krewe of Comus. By the late 1850s, Canal Street had cemented its position as the main street of New Orleans, and ever since it has been an important part of the Carnival season. Comus, Rex, Proteus, Zulu, and all the rest of the city's mythical gods and monarchs have included a swing of their glittering parades on part of the wide main street of the Crescent City.

In 1890 Canal Street was the site of a testy meeting between the parading Mistick Krewe of Comus and the Krewe of Proteus. Comus had not been active for six years, and Proteus had taken over the all-important Mardi Gras nighttime slot. That year, however, Comus decided to make a return trip to the streets. Proteus was not inclined to step aside, with the result that they both rolled at the same time. Proteus reached Canal Street first and took his spin along the uptown side of the wide street, while at about the same time Comus rolled along the downtown side of the street.

The double parade would have certainly added extra excitement to the crowds of people on Canal Street. The neutral ground of Canal Street may have separated the two parades for a while, but they could not remain separated for long, and for a few minutes things were anything but neutral.

The Proteus ball was being held at the French Opera House on Bourbon Street. When the procession reached the intersection of Canal and Bourbon streets, an attempt was made to turn and complete the ride into the French Quarter and the ball. Coincidently, Comus reached the intersection at the same time and wished to continue on his way to the Grand Opera House, part of the site of today's Ritz-Carlton Hotel, where the Comus ball was being held.

The parades abruptly halted and each refused to let the other pass. Threatening glares and angry words were exchanged between the captains, but level heads among gentlemen prevailed when the brother of Proteus' captain intervened.

LYLE SAXON, FROM *FABULOUS NEW ORLEANS* (1928)

On recalling watching Mardi Gras parades as a child around the turn of the twentieth century:

"Canal Street presented a gay picture. There were strings of electric lights looped from corner to corner, and arches of vari-colored electric bulbs crossed the street at close intervals—yellow, green and purple lights. From the balconies and tops of buildings came long streamers of yellow, green and purple bunting, doubly noticeable now by the artificial light. Flags fluttered and the bunting billowed in the evening breeze from the river. Waves of pleasant coolness came to our grateful faces."

Canal Street crowds on Mardi Gras night in 1893. The Henry Clay Monument and the electric tower are in the background. (Courtesy of The Historic New Orleans Collection)

Men in Arab costumes turning from Canal Street onto St. Charles. Research indicates that this Theodore Lilienthal photograph, although dated circa 1866, may actually be of the first Rex parade in 1872. (Courtesy of the Louisiana State Museum)

The Comus parade was permitted to continue unhindered on its way to the Grand Opera House, and then Proteus went on to the French Opera House. The following year Proteus moved back to its usual Monday parade time, and Comus for the next century paraded unhindered on Mardi Gras night. The Comus Ball was first held at the Gaiety Theater on Gravier Street, and then in the early 1870s moved to the Varieties—later called the Grand Opera House—on Canal Street after fire destroyed the Gaiety. The ball was regularly held there until the 1890s when Comus, along with most other krewes, moved to the French Opera House. It burned in 1919.

For well over a century, vast wall-to-wall crowds of people streamed onto Canal Street in order to welcome and honor the city's "royalty." During the nineteenth century, not only was the street filled with people, but every ironwork gallery was lined with spectators trying to catch a glimpse of the processions. The epicenter of Mardi Gras celebrations on Canal Street in the late nineteenth century was the Henry Clay Monument, where huge crowds gathered—at least until the monument was moved to Lafayette Square in 1901.

Artist George Schmidt's interpretation of the first Rex parade in 1872 as it appeared at Canal and St. Charles near that great gathering place of the time, the Henry Clay Monument. Shown wearing a borrowed costume from a production of Shakespeare's Richard III is Lewis Salomon, the first Rex. (Courtesy of George Schmidt and the School of Design)

Mardi Gras maskers walking along Canal Street between St. Charles and Carondelet in 1910. (Courtesy of The Historic New Orleans Collection)

Riders in the Rex parade and spectators near the corner of Canal and Carondelet in the early twentieth Century. (Courtesy of The Historic New Orleans Collection)

Mardi Gras maskers on Canal Street in 1915. (Courtesy of The Historic New Orleans Collection)

Mardi Gras Day, 1941.

Leon Trice photographed this massive crowd assembled on Canal Street for the lighting of the new streetlights on Monday February 24, 1930. KOM on the D. H. Holmes building refers to the Knights of Momus, which would parade on the next Thursday. (Courtesy of The Historic New Orleans Collection)

During Mardi Gras night, loud and rowdy crowds congregated on Canal Street to see the bright displays of electric lights strung along the buildings and to party until late night brought Lent—or sleep. Today, Carnival crowds on Canal Street are not what they once were. Many spectators now head for the tree-lined confines of St. Charles Avenue or the treeless surroundings of the suburban Metairie route while some nighttime revelers head for Bourbon Street.

Not only was Canal Street once mobbed from side to side with revelers and parade watchers, up until about World War II the crowd was a very dressy one. The concentration of blue denim and other casual attire—or lack of it—did not make its appearance at Carnival parades until the last half of the twentieth century. Before this time, women went to parades wearing their long dresses and hats and gloves, while men wore suits, ties, topcoats, and hats as if they were going to the office or church. Honoring the monarch was something taken more seriously in the past than today, with the emphasis on scrambling for nonstop throws.

Canal Street itself dressed up for Carnival. Thanks to Betty Finnin, the City of New Orleans' official city decorator, the lamp posts on the neutral ground sported clown faces during the 1940s and 1950s. Even the department stores got into the act, with D. H. Holmes welcoming krewes by erecting the initials of various parading organizations in lights above the Canal Street entrance to the store.

During the 1980s and into the 1990s, a Mardi Gras Maskathon costume contest was held on the Canal Street neutral ground. Until 1992 Rex toasted his queen at the Boston Club on Canal Street, but that event

The Rex parade is seen passing along Canal Street circa 1906. In the background is the golden dome of the Mercier Building (Maison Blanche Department Store). (Courtesy of The Historic New Orleans Collection)

This view of the Rex parade on Canal Street, looking from Baronne to the river, about 1907 shows throngs of well-dressed parade goers. (Courtesy of The Historic New Orleans Collection)

Canal Street crowds circa 1950. (Courtesy of the New Orleans Public Library)

A Carnival night parade of the 1930s passes the lavishly illuminated facade of Maison Blanche. (Courtesy of The Historic New Orleans Collection)

As this 1912 photograph shows, people dressed up to attend Mardi Gras parades. (Courtesy of The Historic New Orleans Collection)

Frederick W. Evans reigned as Rex in 1923. (Courtesy of The Historic New Orleans Collection)

Harry B. Kelleher, the 1965 King of Carnival, arrives on Canal Street from St. Charles. Note the Pickwick Club on the right. (Photo by Del Hall)

Canal Street has been superceded by the French Quarter as the place to see Mardi Gras costumes, although Canal has had its share of eye-catching outfits. Over the years there have been costume contests, such as the Channel 6 Mask-a-Thon in the 1980s. (Photo by David S. Binnings; courtesy of the New Orleans Public Library)

A Mardi Gras night parade with mule-drawn floats passes near the once familiar signs of Lord's on Baronne Street and Miller Brothers Square Deal Jewelers. Mules were discontinued after 1950. (Courtesy of The Historic New Orleans Collection)

Canal Street has long been the ideal place to watch Mardi Gras parades.

now occurs at the Intercontinental Hotel on St. Charles Street. There is still one mythical figure who chooses to reign supreme over his subjects on Canal Street. That is Endymion, on the Saturday before Mardi Gras. It was once a rather humble Gentilly neighborhood parade, but in 1974 Endymion expanded to become the largest of the season, with celebrity grand marshals. From its annual starting point in Mid-City, the Endymion parade travels for almost the full length of Canal Street.

During the Endymion parade, as well as the parade of Endymion's uptown counterpart, Bacchus, the throngs of spectators on Canal Street reach numbers reminiscent of the 1920s and 1930s. No parade today brings as many people to Canal Street as Endymion, simply because no other parade travels along so much of the street.

For a few years before the start of World War II, the Krewe of NOR— New Orleans Romance—gave Canal Street over to the city's public school children. In those days of segregation, only white school children chose a king and queen to reign over floats representing each school. NOR was on the Saturday afternoon before Mardi Gras, and like every other Mardi Gras parade of the time, wall-to-wall throngs of people politely watched the passing parade of youngsters.

City decorator Betty Finnin was responsible for Carnival decorations on Canal Street from the 1930s into the 1960s. This big clown on the light standard not far from Claiborne Avenue dates from 1947. (Courtesy of The Historic New Orleans Collection)

Betty Finnin was the official decorator for the City of New Orleans from 1933 to 1970. (Courtesy of the New Orleans Public Library)

For Mardi Gras, official city decorator Betty Finnin had the lights on the Canal Street neutral ground painted purple, green, and gold. (Photo by Dorothy Violet Gulledge; courtesy of the New Orleans Public Library)

The Krewe of Endymion is now the only parade whose route is primarily on Canal Street. (Photograph by Mitchel Osborne)

Before World War I, Rex made his annual Mardi Gras arrival in New Orleans via yacht at the foot of Canal Street the day before Mardi Gras. Then a procession wound its way around the business district. In 1987 the custom of the arrival was reinstated as part of a larger package of riverfront events. (Courtesy of The Historic New Orleans Collection)

The arrival of Rex at the foot of Canal Street the day before Mardi Gras circa 1903. Rex arrives with former New Orleans Mayor Joseph Shakspeare. (Courtesy of The Historic New Orleans Collection)

The Mardi Gras season, like Canal Street, has evolved. As old traditions have gone away, new ones have come in. Beginning in 1876 Rex—the Monarch of Mardi Gras—arrived at his Carnival capitol at the foot of Canal Street on Monday, the day before Mardi Gras. In 1879 he arrived on the steamboat *Robert E. Lee,* although in later years he arrived in flag-bedecked splendor aboard the yacht *Stranger.* The Monday event evolved into a lavish water pageant preceding a small procession that wound through the streets of downtown—a grand preparation for the yet bigger parade of the next day. In 1899 Rex boarded his royal chariot at the Canal Street ferry building and was frozen to his throne during the city's worst recorded freeze.

In 1917 the tradition ended, but within our own generation the formal Monday arrival of Rex at Spanish Plaza/Riverwalk at the foot of Canal Street has been reinstated. This was dubbed "Lundi Gras" (Fat Monday) in 1987, and the term, used intermittently in the New Orleans black Creole community through the years, is now a part of everybody's

Rex arriving at his Carnival capital at the foot of Canal Street accompanied by city offi-cials the day before Mardi Gras in 1907. Note the Canal Street ferry building on the left. (Courtesy of Frank Gordon and Bergeron Gallery)

In addition to its original themed floats, the Rex parade also has several "signature floats" that are seen every year. The King's Jester is one of them.

Rex arrives from a Coast Guard buoy tender at Riverwalk. (Photo by Peggy Scott Laborde)

Rex proclaims "It's Carnival Time" on the stage at Riverwalk Marketplace.

A Rex lieutenant on horseback during the parade. Behind him is the Boston Club, one of Canal Street's oldest structures. (Photo by Peggy Scott Laborde)

The route of the Mid-City parade once included most of Canal Street. Known for its floats made of tin foil, Mid-City now uses the St. Charles Avenue route but still turns onto downtown Canal Street. This view is from 1966. (Photo by Dorothy Violet Gulledge; courtesy of the New Orleans Public Library)

lexicon. Lundi Gras helps kick off the climax of the Carnival Season, and this continues to cement Canal Street's historic importance as a central gathering point of Carnival.

Popularity of the name Lundi Gras has given the arrival of Rex additional meaning because of the wide range of events that now occur throughout the day and evening. A prime example is the Monday arrival of King Zulu and his court at nearby Woldenberg Park, helping to begin a day of festivities.

How fitting that much of the very celebration of Carnival that has become so intrinsic to New Orleans continues to include the main street of New Orleans as a backdrop.

CHAPTER TEN

Streetcars

IF ANYTHING PROMOTED Canal Street's evolution into New Orleans' great gathering place, as well as its prime shopping area, it was the way the city's streetcar system grew. Canal Street's great width could easily accommodate tracks of the various lines along its route as well as the tracks from uptown and downtown lines that terminated at the street and then swung around for the return trip.

In 1893 the city's twenty-seven streetcar lines owed their existence as much to the geography of the city as to its culture. Most lines ran parallel to the Mississippi River and along streets only a mile or so back from the river. Since so many lines terminated on Canal Street, it had the greatest concentration of streetcar tracks in the city. Lines for the most part did not cross the street, but by terminating there, further made

Canal Street in the mid-1890s looking from St. Charles shows the many streetcars in the area and the tall tower designed to support the utility wires that crisscrossed the street. (Courtesy of The Historic New Orleans Collection)

A mule-drawn streetcar makes its way around the statue of Henry Clay at the corner of Canal and Royal Streets. (Courtesy of The Historic New Orleans Collection)

Canal Street an ideal place to congregate. Few streetcar lines ran perpendicularly to the river. Canal Street was one of the few exceptions, since its tracks stretched to the cemeteries, and some lines reached even to West End on the shore of Lake Pontchartrain.

Canal Street's position as the merging point for so many streetcar lines did not evolve until about the time of the Civil War, when the street was emerging as a vital retail corridor. Nineteenth-century Canal Street's important centerpiece—the Henry Clay Monument, where Royal Street meets St. Charles Street—had recently been erected, and both coincided with a period of dramatic expansion in the establishment of streetcar lines all over town.

The first public transportation system in New Orleans was a mule- and horse-drawn omnibus line. It operated between the center of town and the terminal of the Pontchartrain Railroad on Elysian Fields Avenue near the Mississippi River. This line was established in 1832, and by the mid-1860s omnibus lines served most of the city, with about a dozen lines in operation. Several of them could be compared to modern airport busses, since they ran between hotels and railroad depots.

By the 1860s cities across the United States were witnessing the construction of mule- and horse-drawn streetcar lines. New Orleans' first street railway—and the world's oldest still-operating streetcar line—was the New Orleans and Carrollton Railroad, which is now the St. Charles streetcar. At the time it was more of a railroad than a streetcar line.

In its early days the St. Charles line terminated at Baronne and Canal streets, not at Carondelet as it does today. By 1860 there were still only four lines serving parts of the uptown area, and they in no way served the entire city. During the next decade, significant expansion occurred as new lines were added to a transportation network that would cover virtually all of the city's urban area.

By the twentieth century, Canal Street had five tracks along its route between the Liberty Monument at the river end and Claiborne Avenue, before extending to the cemeteries. It was not unusual to see rows of streetcars rumbling one after the other along each of these tracks. In an age before automobiles, the traffic jams were made up of streetcars, especially during the morning and evening rush hours.

By the mid-1920s, the New Orleans streetcar system numbered twenty-eight lines and served nearly 150 million passengers annually in a city with a population of roughly 450,000. Most of the lines focused on Canal Street, where people shopped, went to the movies, and attended Carnival parades. Packed streetcars even ran alongside throngs of revelers during the Rex parades.

Early in the twentieth century, automobiles had begun to compete with streetcars as a mode of transportation. During the 1920s, angle parking was allowed on the Canal Street neutral ground. Later, this gave way to parallel parking. Parking along the median was banned in the 1930s. (Courtesy of The Historic New Orleans Collection)

By the early 1880s, electric street cars were appearing in some American cities, and ran as part of a display at the World's Industrial and Cotton Centennial Exposition held in Audubon Park in 1884-85. However, it was not until 1893 that the first electric cars began to appear on a New Orleans transit line.

On February 1, 1893, the St. Charles line was converted to electricity, and beginning in 1896, the line ran for one block along Canal Street, as it does today, to begin its return uptown trip.

By the end of the nineteenth century, nearly all of the transit lines had been electrified, and this resulted in a rapid outward expansion of the city to include fringe residential areas such as Mid-City and Canal Street itself. Coupled with the improved drainage system built after 1899, these areas boomed.

Around the Henry Clay Monument was a junction nicknamed Monkey Wrench Corner where there was a seeming tangle of tracks and mule-drawn cars. The monument was a traffic obstacle from the time it was erected, and the coming of the electric cars made the situation even more difficult.

In 1895 the base of the monument was reduced to help make way for the new track arrangement, but finally in 1901 the monument was moved to Lafayette Square, where it still stands.

Prior to 1922 the New Orleans streetcar network was made up of numerous independently owned lines. One such line was the Canal Line, originally operated by the New Orleans City Railroad Company. The

Streetcar conductors such as Joseph Wyndham Bordelon found themselves on Canal Street for all or part of their routes.

line went into operation on June 15, 1861, and at first ran out Canal from St. Charles to North White Street, where its barn was located. But a few months later it was extended out to the cemeteries, ending at the Half Way House, a popular stop for refreshments and music on the New Basin Canal at Metairie Road.

The Canal line was electrified in 1894. Another line was the Canal Belt, which operated from 1901 to 1934. It ran from the foot of Canal Street out to City Park Avenue and looped back downtown via Esplanade Avenue and North Rampart Street. These lines helped draw new residents to a neighborhood that would come to be called Mid-City.

The Desire streetcar is seen here in the 700 block of Canal Street in the 1940s as it turns onto Bourbon Street for its return trip. (Photo by Gene Leingang; courtesy of Bergeron Gallery)

The streetcar strike of 1929 was marked by violence. On July 5 a streetcar was toppled and burned near the Algiers ferry ramp at the foot of Canal Street. The Liberty Place Monument is visible here at its original location. (Courtesy of The Historic New Orleans Collection)

As the twentieth century progressed, one streetcar line after the other was replaced by motorized busses. The rather inauspicious Desire streetcar line, which turned along Canal Street as it looped back from Royal to Bourbon Street, was immortalized in 1947 as probably the most famous streetcar line in the world when Tennessee Williams' Pulitzer Prize-winning play, "A Streetcar Named Desire," premiered in New York. The following year, the Desire streetcar line ceased to exist when it was replaced by a bus line. Before the inspiration of this streetcar, Williams was considering calling his play "The Poker Night." Timing is everything.

In the years immediately after World War I, streetcar usage increased, and reached record levels by the middle-1920s; however, the growing use of electric and motor busses and private automobiles began whittling away at streetcar service. The automobile was first displayed in New Orleans in 1899, and within twenty short years Canal Street was lined with diagonally parked cars, not only along the sidewalks but along the neutral ground as well.

As traffic congestion became more of a problem, parallel parking was instituted. Eventually, parking along the neutral ground was prohibited. Automobiles soon became the transportation norm for people living in the city and especially for the ever-increasing number of residents commuting from growing suburbia.

Strikes did little to enhance public transportation. The actions created public disruptions and caused much inconvenience for working people. But once the strikes ended, streetcar usage returned to normal levels since this was the only form of transportation available to most people prior to the automobile age. This was not necessarily the case during the especially violent streetcar strike of 1929. Commuters quickly learned to car pool and to employ any form of jitney transit in order to get to work downtown. Along Canal Street things were much more frustrating, since the street was in the midst of a major repaving and beautification project.

The strike began on July 1, 1929, over the unwillingness of New Orleans Public Service to accept a closed-shop provision for workers and to limit its right to readily fire personnel. The strike was especially violent, and included the dynamiting of a manager's house uptown on Magazine Street. Women posed throwing rocks at the Arabella Street car barn. Vehicles were burned, and Canal Street became a focal point of this activity when a streetcar was ceremoniously set aflame in front of a huge

In this view from Canal Street toward the Mississippi River, people are carpooling and riding jitney taxis during the 1929 streetcar strike. At the time, Canal Street was being repaved. (Courtesy of The Historic New Orleans Collection)

A citizens' group called Streetcars Desired Inc. tried in vain to save the Canal streetcar from being discontinued in 1964. When the line returned forty years later, many of the group's members took the first ride. (Photo by Del Hall)

The bright red and yellow-trimmed Canal streetcar returned to service in April 2004. Running from the Mississippi River to the cemeteries, the line has a spur that enables some cars to travel down North Carrollton Avenue as far as City Park. (Courtesy of Peggy Scott Laborde)

crowd near the Algiers ferry ramp. Things gradually returned to normal, beginning on August 15, 1929, but the number of streetcar riders never returned to those levels reached prior to the mid-1920s.

By 1964 there were two operating streetcar lines in New Orleans—St. Charles Avenue and Canal Street. On May 31, 1964, at 5 A.M. busses replaced the Canal streetcars. With the exception of one block between Carondelet and St. Charles streets to allow the St. Charles Avenue street-car to turn around, the neutral ground from Claiborne Avenue to Front Street was paved over, and tracks were ripped up to serve the new busses. As Louis Hennick and E. Harper Charlton wrote in 1975 in *The Streetcars of New Orleans,* "The world-wide image of Canal Street has been severely altered. . . . The disappearance of the streetcars has torn the heart out of Canal Street's image."

Streetcars were not considered progressive by many people, and city government and most of the local media either supported the conversion to busses or just remained mute on the issue. A citizens' group, "Streetcars Desired Inc.," tried in vain to save the line.

The Canal streetcar line returned almost thirty years later. In 2004, in the early hours of a cool April morning, around 3 A.M., streetcar fans and other folks, many of whom had tried to save the original line, boarded the streetcars while cheering the return of something that had been such an essential part of the street's magic. The new Canal streetcar is air-conditioned, handicapped accessible, and bright red with yellow trim. If Canal Street can be compared to one long table, these streetcars are the long-stemmed American Beauty roses in the center.

After little more than a year in operation, the Canal streetcars were flooded by the 17th Street levee break during Hurricane Katrina. They remained out of service for an extended period.

The Louisville and Nashville Railway Station was located near the foot of Canal Street and the Algiers ferry ramp. An L&N station had been on this site since the early 1870s and was demolished in the 1950s after the Union Passenger Terminal was built. (Courtesy of The Historic New Orleans Collection)

CHAPTER ELEVEN

Trains

FOR MUCH OF the history of New Orleans, people came to and from the city via water—either the Mississippi River or Lake Pontchartrain. In the movie version of *Gone With the Wind,* Rhett and Scarlett Butler journey to the city in the late 1860s for their honeymoon aboard a Mississippi riverboat. With this longtime dependence on the river for transportation, it was only fitting that in the years prior to World War I Rex, the King of Carnival, made his arrival in New Orleans the day before Mardi Gras on the Mississippi River. Since 1987 this arrival on the mighty Mississippi has been reinstated as part of the Lundi Gras festivities.

Although two of the earliest railroads in the United States were established in New Orleans in the 1830s, they were short lines. The St. Charles and Carrollton Railroad extended only to Carrollton along modern St. Charles Avenue, and the Pontchartrain Railroad traveled out Elysian Fields Avenue to Lake Pontchartrain. As to the establishment of interstate rail lines, Louisiana was rather late in the process, and by the mid-1850s just about the farthest one could travel from the Crescent City by rail was to Jackson, Mississippi.

Beginning after the Civil War, the state's rail connections began to expand dramatically; in the early 1870s, one could travel by train between New Orleans and Mobile. By the end of that decade, the city was connected to most places north and east, and Los Angeles could be reached via the Southern Pacific Railroad.

By the last decades of the nineteenth century, more and more people were arriving in New Orleans by rail, and this mode of travel was fast replacing riverboat travel. Eighty years after Scarlett and Rhett came to the Crescent City by steamboat, Blanche DuBois in "A Streetcar Named Desire" steps onto Canal Street from a railroad station. By 1947 when the play premiered in New York, the railroad, while still the chief method of travel in the United States, was beginning to be replaced by airline travel. The change would bring about the end of railroad stations. At just about the same time, the Desire streetcar line, which passed on Canal Street as it turned off Royal Street onto Bourbon, became a bus line.

For the first half of the twentieth century, just about every famous person to visit New Orleans came via train and got off at one of its stations. One of the famous visitors of the 1920s was Izzy Einstein, one of the best-known federal Prohibition agents of the day. In 1923 he toured large

American cities in an informal "contest" to see where he could find a drink the fastest. New Orleans won. When he left his railway station, he got into a taxi and asked the driver where he could obtain a drink. The driver pulled a bottle out from under the seat. The time it took was thirty-five seconds.

For some railway travelers, including Blanche Dubois, their first glimpse of New Orleans was of the bright lights of Canal Street. At the height of rail travel in the United States during the first half of the twentieth century, there were five railroad stations in New Orleans. Two of them were at either end of the business section of Canal Street. The Louisville and Nashville Station was near the river, while the Southern Railway Terminal was on Basin Street.

The local predecessor of the Louisville and Nashville Railroad was the New Orleans and Mobile Railroad that connected the two cities by 1870. This occurred only after the bridging of bayous, bays, and swamps made possible by some impressive feats of engineering. The L&N terminal began as a little wood frame cottage on the French Quarter side of Canal Street and was wedged in between the open wharves of the riverfront and the sugar sheds on Wells Street right off Canal. By the 1890s the New Orleans and Mobile had been absorbed by the L&N, and a larger terminal was constructed at the site of the previous one. It was still anything but grand, consisting of a ticket office and a covered platform set amidst the many railroad tracks which by then had proliferated along the city's riverfront.

The Louisville and Nashville Station became one of the busiest in New Orleans, partly because it was from here that New Orleanians were able to leave for one of their favorite vacation haunts, the Mississippi Gulf Coast. For some people, it had already become a daily commuter stop as early as the 1880s, since some New Orleans businessmen had begun living permanently in Waveland and Bay St. Louis. The scheduled railroad trip took only about ninety minutes.

In 1901 a new Louisville and Nashville Station replaced the old platform. Built in the Richardsonian style, it was a red brick structure adorned with a low corner tower topped with a pointed roof. Adjacent to

The Louisville and Nashville Railway Station, seen here circa 1910, was a landmark near the river end of Canal Street. It was demolished in the 1950s. (Courtesy of The Historic New Orleans Collection)

The Southern Railway Terminal on the Basin Street neutral ground was designed by noted Chicago architect Daniel Burnham and built in 1908. It was demolished in the late 1950s after becoming obsolete when the Union Passenger Terminal opened. (Courtesy of The Historic New Orleans Collection)

the building was an elaborate arched train shed that stretched several hundred feet alongside and beyond the main terminal building into the riverfront section of the French Quarter. The L&N also handled massive export traffic and had extensive freight yards that reached several blocks back from the wharves and cut across Canal Street as far upriver as Julia Street.

Surrounded by so many railroad tracks and warehouses, the Louisville and Nashville Station was not in a particularly glamorous section of Canal Street. In the 1920s a viaduct was built along Canal Street to the Algiers ferry landing. The viaduct obscured the facade of the terminal. In spite of its location, the station still offered one of the best views of the beacons and towers of the downtown skyline a few blocks away—and this view was seen every day by the many commuters who made their way to Canal Street aboard the Algiers ferry.

The other Canal Street station was about ten blocks away on Basin Street's neutral ground, or median. A railroad had existed there since about 1880, but it was only a short line, going out to the Spanish Fort Amusement Park near the mouth of Bayou St. John. The line had a rather unprepossessing one-story frame station on Canal Street. It was then on the fringes of the business district, and just behind its Basin Street tracks and sheds was the legendary Storyville red-light district. Storyville's heyday was from 1897, when the city authorized its opening, until 1917, when the U.S. secretary of the navy initiated its closure. All of the city's railroad stations were prime locations for selling the "Blue Book"—that handy little guide advertising the madams, houses, and other businesses of Storyville.

By the twentieth century, the station was serving interstate passengers via the Gulf and Mobile Railroad and the Northern and Southern Railroad. In 1908 the monumental Southern Railway Station was opened on the site. It was designed by Chicago architect Daniel Burnham, a leader in the City Beautiful movement. He attracted national attention for his plans to redesign San Francisco and Chicago, as well as oversee the design and construction of the latter city's 1893 World's Fair.

In New Orleans in 1902 he designed the Hibernia Bank Building on Carondelet and Gravier streets. Later it was called the Carondelet Building. It is now the Hampton Inn. This structure is not to be confused with today's much taller Hibernia National Bank Building built in 1921.

By 1908 the Canal Street business district was growing toward the Southern Railway Terminal, which provided people arriving through this impressive terminal a much more exciting urban outlook of Canal Street than would be offered near the Louisville and Nashville Station. For a few years the Southern station stood out among mostly older townhouses that were being turned into businesses. In 1903 the Krauss Department Store—that shopping venue popular with the ladies of Storyville—was built on the lake side of Basin Street. During the next half century, it would grow to fill the entire block.

By 1930 passengers alighting from the Southern station could see less than a block away the bright marquees of the first-run Loew's State Theatre and Saenger Theatre. Although out of sight, the Orpheum Theater on University Place and the Strand Theater on Baronne Street were only about two blocks away. In the Saenger building was the LaSalle Hotel, while a short distance across Canal Street from the station were the new Jung Hotel and the Hotel New Orleans. Visible in the opposite direction was the tall, venerable Grunewald—later the Roosevelt and now the Fairmont—Hotel. Stretching from Krauss toward the river were block after block of signs, awnings, show windows, and neon signs proclaiming the South's premier shopping district.

In 1952 both train stations became obsolete after only about half a century of service when the new Union Passenger Station opened on Loyola Avenue. The new facility consolidated many of the lines from the city's other railroad stations. In the late 1950s, both the Louisville and Nashville Station and the Southern Railway Terminal met the same fate of demolition. The L&N site became a utility service area, while the Southern Railway Terminal was replaced by a long, grassy stretch honoring the heroes of Latin American independence. The monument to Simon Bolivar serves as a reminder of the 1950s and 1960s when New Orleans was called the Gateway to the Americas.

Across the street from Simon Bolivar is Molly Marine, a rather diminutive statue standing on Elk Place. It was dedicated in 1943 as the first monument to women members of the Armed Forces in the United States. Originally from Mexico, prolific New Orleans-based artist Enrique Alferez was the statue's creator. In a career that spanned over half a century, Alferez produced work that can be seen all over New Orleans, especially in City Park.

What was once the less glamorous station site, the Louisville and Nashville Station, on the river side of Canal Street, is now the center of the downtown tourist trade, offering Harrah's Casino, the Aquarium of the Americas, luxury hotels, and some of the region's finest and most fashionable shopping.

The whistle from the Public Belt Railroad running up and down the harbor of the Port of New Orleans is all that is left of any railroad activity. One longtime railway fan, pondering the fate of the original Canal streetcar and the two train stations and the vitality they helped to create, was prompted to observe: "There's nothing like the rolling wheel!"

Throughout most of the history of Storyville, from 1897 to 1917, "Blue Books" advertising the houses and other businesses of the infamous red-light district were sold at train stations and various other locations in New Orleans. Most "Blue Book" covers were not illustrated, which makes this example from about 1900 unusual. (Courtesy of The Historic New Orleans Collection)

Custom House
1840

The second Custom House, this one designed by Benjamin Buisson.

CHAPTER TWELVE
The Custom House

AN IMPORTANT ANCHOR near the river end of Canal Street is the United States Custom House. Since the time of the Spanish occupation of Louisiana in the late eighteenth century, there has been a customhouse where the current massive building stands. The earlier customhouses did not occupy the entire square, and during the eighteenth and early nineteenth centuries the buildings were on the riverfront prior to the subdivision of the batture between the levee and the river.

The Spanish *Duan* was originally a tobacco warehouse with a customs shed, and the street behind it was called *Rua Duane,* which was later translated to Customhouse Street, ultimately to be renamed Iberville Street in 1903.

Jay Dearborn Edwards' photograph of Canal Street in the late 1850s shows the scaffolding surrounding the Custom House, which had been under construction for about ten years. (Courtesy of The Historic New Orleans Collection)

The Custom House has housed the records of port activities, ships, cargoes, port procedures, and regulations. During the American period, three Custom House buildings have occupied the site. Each building was larger than its predecessor, reflecting the growing importance of the port of New Orleans during the nineteenth century.

The first American Custom House was built in 1809 from designs by Benjamin H. B. Latrobe, English-born designer of the first part of the United States Capitol Building. The building was a modest structure of red brick trimmed with stone, and it had green shutters. Its foundation and design were not well suited to New Orleans terrain, and the building was demolished only ten years after it opened. A larger, yet still modest structure designed by Benjamin Buisson replaced it. The new building was located near the middle of the block. Soon after, it was joined on the block by the Mariners' Church, which served the many seamen who came through the city's port.

In 1848 both buildings were pulled down for a new, larger, and grander Custom House befitting the importance of New Orleans. Designed by Alexander T. Wood and with construction superintended by Thomas K. Wharton, the massive building, with its four sides not parallel, features Greek Corinthian columns on Roman bases surmounted by Egyptian lotus capitals. Although begun in the late 1840s, construction was interrupted by the Civil War, and the cast-iron cornice was not added until about 1880.

North Peters and Decatur streets, photographed from the top of the Custom House by Jay Dearborn Edwards in the late 1850s. This view shows at right the levee and wharves that had once been part of the river batture. (Courtesy of The Historic New Orleans Collection)

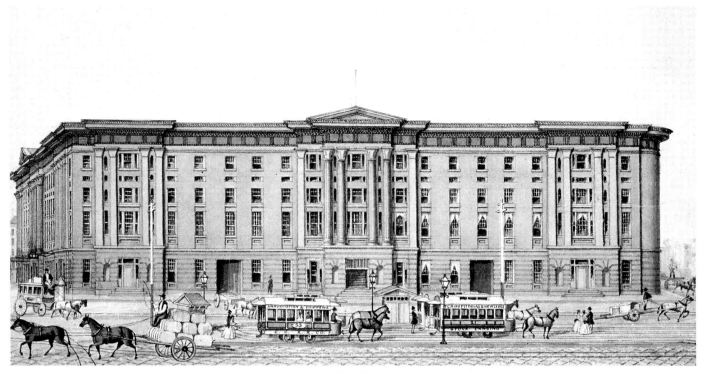

One of Marie Adrien Persac's views of the Custom House in 1873. Persac showed the finished building, although its cast-iron cornice was not added until about 1880. (Courtesy of The Historic New Orleans Collection)

With the beginning of the Civil War, most of the building was complete and already serving as the city's main post office. It continued as such until 1906 when a new post office opened on Camp Street at Lafayette Square. During the war, the Custom House first served the Confederacy as a shell and gun-carriage factory. After the city fell in April 1862, the building became a Union prison.

Days before New Orleans surrendered to the Union, T. K. Wharton, who was a Confederate sympathizer and was saddened by the fall of the city, went to the top of his beloved Custom House where he had "a clear view of 5 Federal War ships." He continued to visit the Custom House regularly to "see that all was right there, as in these dangerous times I shall adhere to my post of duty to the last." On another trip to the Custom House he found it "taken possession of by the Federal officers with a large fleet of war steamers to sustain them [and] I could transact no business." He took his son to see the quartered United States troops, which he reckoned to number about 1,000. Wharton went again "to the Custom House & the City Hall and found both occupied by large bodies of Federal troops, to whom I had nothing to say."

At the time it was built, the Custom House was the largest U.S. government building outside of Washington, D.C. It was the heaviest building constructed in New Orleans, and for decades was the biggest building on Canal Street. Constructed in an age before skyscrapers came to be supported by massive concrete foundations, the Custom House is held up

The grand staircase of the Custom House, seen in this 1892 view, is one of the finest in the city. (Courtesy of The Historic New Orleans Collection)

The Custom House as it appeared in 1892. (Courtesy of The Historic New Orleans Collection)

on a grillage, a framework of one-foot-thick timber and concrete—not cotton bales, as some people mistakenly believe. As the Custom House neared completion in 1861, Wharton wrote that "The Building when completed will be the most Capacious, Carefully Constructed and best arranged Commercial Structure in the United States."

During the 1920s, as the center of Federal activities in New Orleans, the Custom House became the focal point of the often difficult enforcement of national Prohibition in New Orleans. For the first several years of Prohibition, the city remained relatively wide open as it overlooked the law whenever possible. In 1925 this resulted in one of the most ambitious raids of speakeasies and other establishments dispensing illegal alcohol.

Federal agents were sent to New Orleans from all over the country to take part in what was until then the biggest raid of the Prohibition era. Virtually every speakeasy, as well as the French Quarter entertainment zone called the Tango Belt along and near Iberville Street, was shut down. Most of the confiscated liquor was transported to the Custom House, and agents declared that they had never seen so much liquor in their lives. Bottles and boxes filled every hallway, office, and nook of the proud and stately Canal Street building.

Many men of a certain age still have vivid memories of going to the Custom House for a military draft physical. Where soldiers once stood, new soldiers were being made.

Marie Adrien Persac's 1873 drawing of the ornate cast-iron waterworks building on the Canal Street neutral ground near the river. The building was used as a free market during the Civil War and was demolished in the early 1870s. The New Orleans and Mobile Railroad Station is at the far right. (Courtesy of The Historic New Orleans Collection)

CHAPTER THIRTEEN
The River End

THE SPOT WHERE Canal Street meets the Mississippi River at what is now called Spanish Plaza has not always been land. Once the area between Tchoupitoulas and North Peters streets and the Mississippi River was part of the river itself, or its batture—silt deposited by the flowing water. The batture was submerged during flood season but relatively dry the rest of the year.

That portion of the riverfront was slowly silted over during the city's first century of existence. The process was helped along by docked ships and barges and wharves that slowed the water, allowing silt to be dropped. Purposely driven poles helped deposit even more silt and build up more dry ground. Indeed, by the early nineteenth century the batture was mostly dry ground, and when protected by levees, was ready for building.

For several decades this new land was embroiled in ongoing litigation. A pamphlet war, which was entered into even by Thomas Jefferson, tried to determine who actually possessed the rights to the Mississippi River banks at the beginning of what would become the Canal Street batture. By the 1840s the case had been settled in favor of several owners, and

Harrah's Casino, which opened in the late 1990s, added to the street life of Canal Street at the river end. The casino was designed by the architectural firm of Perez, Ernst, Farnet. (Courtesy of Harrah's Casino)

"No visit to New Orleans is complete without a trip on the steamer President."

—promotional flyer from the 1950s

For anyone walking up the ramp either for the afternoon tour of the harbor or for the nightly dance, the smell of coffee beans from a nearby warehouse was a reminder that the Port of New Orleans could easily mix business with pleasure.

During the 1950s and early 1960s, a moonlight cruise that included bouncy jazz-filled tunes from the Crawford-Ferguson Night Owls Band was a highlight of the New Orleans nightlife scene. Leading this jazz revival group were trombonist Paul Crawford and drummer Len Ferguson.

With five decks and a two-deck-tall ballroom, and nearly a football

The steamer President.

175

Performing for the steamer President*'s dance trips during the 1950s and into the 1960s was the Crawford-Ferguson Night Owls.*

field in length, the *President* was well suited as a musical setting. It could accommodate 1,000 dancers and seat 1,500 for a concert. The boat was owned by the Streckfus family who went into the excursion boat business in the early 1900s and remained active for over three-quarters of a century.

"They only sold set-ups, so if you wanted liquor you could bring it, which made the evening even less expensive." recalls clarinetist and jazz historian Jack Stewart. "The Night Owls played New Orleans jazz, and it was a really nice thing if you wanted to get a whole group of people together. I must have gone forty or fifty times on the *President.*"

Stewart, a founding member of the New Leviathan Oriental Foxtrot Orchestra, also knew what it was like to play on the vessel. "The dance floor would kind of really vibrate, and with the dancers and your playing, you were in touch with the rhythm of the music and the rhythm of the dancers."

During the 1970s and 1980s, nighttime concerts sponsored by the New Orleans Jazz and Heritage Festival were held on board. "The *President* was one of the greatest venues ever," recalls music writer/cartoonist Bunny Matthews,

because if you didn't like the

Eads Plaza was beautifully landscaped in this early 1960s photo. Note the steamer President *docked nearby. (Photo by Dorothy Violet Gulledge; courtesy of the New Orleans Public Library)*

subdivision and commercial development of the land quickly followed. Today, the batture supports some of the most important projects in the city, such as the Riverwalk Festival Marketplace, the World Trade Center, Canal Place, the Windsor Court Hotel, and Harrah's Casino.

The riverfront was once one of the most important gathering places in New Orleans. Here, visitors arrived by riverboat and local residents went out to promenade. On the riverfront one could not only take advantage of cool river breezes, but also experience the incessant hustle and bustle of one of the world's great ports and see trading goods such as sugar and cotton that helped produce the wealth of New Orleans.

For nearly two centuries, the whole city was open to the river. During the eighteenth and early nineteenth centuries, the harbor was a bare levee along which vessels docked and on which unprotected merchandise was unloaded. By the late 1850s, a wide plank wharf had been built parallel to the levee extending for miles up and down the river.

Starting in the 1860s, a network of railroad tracks was built near the river alongside industries and large warehouses. After the establishment of the New Orleans Port Commission in 1896, an ambitious program of building new wharves with large covered sheds was undertaken. While this modernized the port, it also cut the city off from the river, leaving few places in the built-up part of town where people could readily see the mighty Mississippi.

One spot, however, where one could appreciate the Mississippi was the foot of Canal Street. During the great river flood of 1927—when the levee was blown up below New Orleans to relieve pressure on the city—downtown office workers and shop clerks streamed to the foot of Canal Street during their lunch hours to gaze in awe at the unusually high water.

Here, in the first half of the twentieth century, was Eads Plaza, named for James Buchanan Eads. He was the man who first bridged the Mississippi at St. Louis. Locally, he was responsible for designing the jetties at the mouth of the Mississippi that prevent the build up of silt and the making of sand bars. This insured that ships could pass and thus saved the great port of New Orleans. *The WPA Guide to New Orleans* in 1938 observed that "facing toward the city [from Eads Plaza] one has a magnificent view of Canal Street. . . . On each side, the crowded buildings of the business section pile up against the sky . . ."

It was at the foot of Canal Street off Eads Plaza where excursion and entertainment boats docked as an important part of the river scene in New Orleans. Among the most memorable of these were steamers of the Streckfus Line such as *Capitol* and *Sydney*. In the 1920s some of New Orleans' most famous jazz musicians, including Warren "Baby" Dodds, Johnny Dodds, and New Orleans' most internationally famous ambassador of music, Louis Armstrong, played on those boats. For many years during the mid-twentieth century, the steamboat *President* docked at the foot of Canal Street.

Eads Plaza was the location of the building that had been constructed around 1930 to house the offices of the Board of Port Commissioners. The plaza was embellished about the same time with a balustrade, steps, and a concrete platform, while the ends of the adjoining wharves were finished to resemble the board building.

Eads Plaza was redeveloped in the mid-1960s when it was incorporated into the grounds of the International Trade Mart, now the World Trade Center. It was renamed Spanish Plaza in recognition of a gift from the Spanish government to rebuild the plaza with tiles and a central

The International Trade Mart (the World Trade Center) and the Rivergate, seen here in the late 1960s, were the beginning of the modernization of the riverfront portion of Canal Street.

music you could go outside and watch the Mississippi River go by and look at the architecture of New Orleans. There were many great concerts there. The B-52s, I remember, was a really fantastic show, and Muddy Waters. So they had all kinds of stuff going on.

When the *President* was undergoing maintenance, it was replaced by an Art Deco floating palace called the *Admiral*, also a part of the Streckfus fleet. With its sleek steel hull, it almost seemed futuristic. Post-parade Mardi Gras parties presented by the Contemporary Arts Center's and "Krewe of Clones" were held on the vessel in the early 1980s. During one of those parties, a group of revelers dressed as bees were aghast when a besotted member of the "hive" jumped from the mezzanine to the dance floor. Fortunately, a sprained ankle was the extent of this queen bee's injury.

But it is the *President* that most locals remember. Built in 1924 as the steam packet boat *Cincinnati*, it was acquired by the St. Louis-based Streckfus Lines five years later. As a packet boat, the vessel carried passengers and freight from Cincinnati to Louisville. Its first trip to New Orleans was for Mardi Gras. By the 1930s it had become a full-time excursion boat, with New Orleans its home for the fall and winter and St. Louis its address during the rest of the year. In 1941 it took up permanent residence in New Orleans.

Before the *President*, the *S.S. Capitol* was docked at the foot of Canal Street. It was also owned by the Streckfus family. Capt. Joe

Streckfus hired the legendary black pianist Fate Marable to assemble jazz bands for his fleet. "We were going in and out of New Orleans all the time," recalled Marable, "and the music was really getting under my skin."

The late New Orleans jazz bass pianist Sherwood Mangiapane remembers his days as a very young passenger on the riverboats.

My mother and father were young enough then to dance and used to like to go on the *Capitol.* I was a little boy and my mother and father had to take me on there when they went. But all they had to do was put me by the band and they could go anywhere they wanted to on that boat. Come back and I'd be in the same place, just standing there listening to the band.

A young Louis Armstrong remembers hearing Marable play the calliope:

I used to go to the foot of Canal Street—out there by the L&N [Train] Station—and just sit there listening to Fate Marable swing those calliope keys down to a low gravy. And—not with the slightest intentions or knowledge that I would be featured trumpet in his famous orchestra. It just goes to show you—it's a small and beautiful world.

In 1919 Marable heard Armstrong play and invited the young musician to join him on the riverboat *Sidney.* "Armstrong all but set the boat on fire with his playing," said Marable. "Captain Joe was a real jazz fan

The development of Riverwalk Marketplace was made possible by the use of buildings that were constructed for the 1984 World's Fair.

In the 1920s a long ramp was built along Canal Street to the Algiers ferry landing. The ferry served many daily commuters who traveled from Algiers across the river to work or to shop. (Courtesy of The Historic New Orleans Collection)

fountain. The old port building was demolished, and the board is now housed at a new location further upriver. The Spanish Plaza has become not only the focal point of the Riverwalk Festival Marketplace, a shopping mall that includes the old Poydras Street Wharf, but also a gathering place for festive events, such as Lundi Gras.

From the time that the first steamboat arrived in New Orleans in 1812, steam ferries have been a part of the cityscape, and one of the oldest, most famous, and most heavily used is the Canal Street/Algiers ferry. At one time there were six ferry lines connecting the east and west banks of the city, and until the opening of the Huey P. Long Bridge in 1935, that was the only way to cross the river at New Orleans. Even railroad cars were carried across the river on giant ferries such as the *Mastodon*.

Several ferry buildings over the years were located at the foot of Canal Street. In the 1850s such buildings were little more than framed cottages, but by the 1880s there was a more substantial structure, adorned by a tall clock tower topped by a powerful electric light. By the 1890s this building had been replaced by a somewhat more ornate structure with an ornamental roof and low clock tower.

Part of this building was blown down during the 1915 hurricane. By the 1920s this building was gone, and a long viaduct was constructed to carry pedestrians to the ferry. In the days before general automobile ownership and bridges across the river, the Algiers ferry carried large numbers of commuters on their way to downtown jobs every day. Although not as heavily used today, the Algiers ferry still offers one of the most spectacular views of the downtown New Orleans skyline.

The foot of Canal Street is one of the most dynamic and high-profile sections of modern New Orleans. There are fashionable shops at Canal Place and the Riverwalk, all within walking distance of some of the city's finest hotels. All of this is anchored by tourist attractions such as the

Commuters from the Algiers ferry going to work downtown or to shop on Canal Street. (Courtesy of The Historic New Orleans Collection)

at heart," noted Armstrong, and the lineup of who played on Steckfus steamers reads like a who's who among early jazz pioneers—Johnny St. Cyr, Johnny and Warren "Baby" Dodds, Peter Bocage, A. J. Piron, and Steve Lewis. Armstrong played on the *Capitol* and other Streckfus-owned steamers up and down the Mississippi from 1918 to 1922. It was on these boats that he received a more formal training in music.

According to Dr. Bruce Raeburn, who heads Tulane University's Hogan Jazz Archive,

> New Orleans musicians used to say that playing in Marable's band was going to the conservatory, and I think that probably sums it up. What Marable was, was a taskmaster who was aware of the influence of hot music and sought to incorporate it into his society-band sound, and to some extent he spiced up his bands; but what the musicians got in return was a very able teacher who would not allow any sluffing off. But in most cases they played a variety of dance music which could have included waltzes, schottisches, but also what ultimately becomes the fox-trot.

Armstrong even met legendary trumpeter Bix Biederbecke on one cruise out of Davenport, Iowa. The few hours that Armstrong had to himself on the boats were put to good use. He spent a lot of his time on the top deck near the calliope.

"Sit up there in the shade and move around with the sun, stay in the shade and play his horn and listen and calculate and play riffs, practice, learn how to build up an ending. He had more than three years time to do that on that boat in the solitude," observed legendary jazz musician and historian Danny Barker, who played with Armstrong.

According to Raeburn,

I think it probably satisfied Armstrong's wanderlust maybe to the point where it was sated. Because we know when he accepted a telegram and position with Joe "King" Oliver in Chicago, his statement was, "That's the only man I would have left town for." I think is was a safe way to see the world, first fledgling steps out of the cradle, so to speak, so I think what it did was broaden Armstrong's horizons.

And the Streckfus Steamboat Line certainly broadened America's musical horizons by spreading a new sound up the Mississippi that would eventually reach far beyond.

In 1978 the *President*'s side-wheels were removed and replaced by diesel engines. It was sold and left New Orleans in 1988, finding new life for the next decade as a gambling boat in Davenport, Iowa, as part of the Isle of Capri Casino operations. No longer in use as a casino, the boat has been acquired by a steamboat fan who plans to use it for special events.

The Algiers ferry on a recent foggy afternoon. (Courtesy of Peggy Scott Laborde)

The Aquarium of the Americas is located where a wharf once stood alongside industries, warehouses, and railroad tracks.

The Dr. Tichenor Building, as photographed by Charles L. Franck Photographers circa 1920, was located on a triangular block where Canal Street met Common Street. Harrah's Casino now stands on the site. (Courtesy of The Historic New Orleans Collection)

Aquarium of the Americas and Harrah's Casino. This indeed represents change, especially since the lower end of Canal Street was formerly part of the city's industrial and transportation corridor notable for its railroad tracks and warehouses.

Between the 1870s and 1912, a huge sugar refinery operated a block off Canal Street behind modern Canal Place. With only a few buildings remaining, this former center of the New Orleans sugar trade is now covered with parking lots serving the shoppers and visitors to the shops and entertainment spots along the downtown and French Quarter riverfront.

On the neutral ground, or median, between modern Canal Place and

An aerial view of the Rivergate, New Orleans' first convention/exhibition center. (Courtesy of The Historic New Orleans Collection)

The newly built Rivergate in the late 1960s, with the International Trade Mart, then the tallest building on Canal Street, looming in the background.

Harrah's Casino, there was for about a decade a highly ornamented waterworks that was never used for that purpose. Built in 1859, this decorative structure was able to hold 175,000 gallons of water. At the start of the Civil War in 1861 the waterworks was the site of a free market where surplus food was distributed when there were critical food shortages due to the Union blockade. Following the war, the building was vacant. Rusted and dilapidated, it was demolished in 1874.

For decades the surrounding area was filled with small factories, wholesale dealers, and saloons. During the 1950s, there were Greek bars, sailors' hang-outs, low-end retailers, as well as pawnshops and army supply dealers. One of the more memorable pawnshops in New Orleans was Abe's, which was in the original Godchaux's Building near the corner of Chartres Street where the Marriott Hotel now stands.

Some of the old businesses on lower Canal Street grew prosperous and famous. One of them was Dr. Tichenor's Antiseptic Co. Still going strong, Dr. Tichenor's was once produced in a small, mid-nineteenth century building on a triangular block where Common Street once merged into Canal Street. The building, which was demolished in the 1960s, was on part of the site of the Rivergate Exhibition Center where today's Harrah's Casino stands.

Beginning in the 1960s, some of the biggest projects in downtown New Orleans began to materialize along lower Canal Street, and these would leave only a handful of the nineteenth century buildings. Among the first of these new projects were the International Trade Mart and Rivergate exhibition facility, both of which were built during the middle 1960s. The name of the former was changed to the World Trade Center. The Rivergate, one of the most noteworthy and respected modern designs of its time and the city's first convention center, lasted barely three decades before being replaced by Harrah's, the city's first land-based casino.

Tourism is now the dominant factor in the economy of New Orleans, and this is now evident along lower Canal Street. Upscale stores, the Aquarium of the Americas, the casino, and luxury hotels and condominiums now occupy a riverfront space once relegated to busy wharves, warehouses, and shipping services, most of which have either closed or moved.

The tallest of the late twentieth century projects to be found on lower Canal Street are the forty-two-story Marriott Hotel, built in the early 1970s, and the forty-seven-story Sheraton Hotel, completed in 1985. These buildings face each other across Canal Street and dominate the skyline. They also stand on former sites of wholesale dealers, pawnshops, and bars that not long ago were housed in buildings that had barely changed since the nineteenth century.

CHAPTER FOURTEEN
Beyond Downtown: Mid-City

As CANAL STREET extends beyond downtown, it intersects Mid-City. And while that name may seem to imply the geographical center of New Orleans, not so. The name was the winning entry of a contest Hibernia Bank sponsored in the 1920s for what to call their new branch on the corner of Canal and Carrollton Avenue. The winning entry was actually meant to describe an area deemed midway on Canal between the Mississippi River and Lake Pontchartrain.

Until the twentieth century, the urban area of New Orleans was mostly near the Mississippi River. This land was the natural levee, or silt deposited over the centuries by Mississippi River floods, and provided the city with its highest elevations of up to about ten feet above sea level. Inland from the riverfront toward Lake Pontchartrain, elevations decreased steadily to as much as eight feet below sea level. Elevations then increase to a few feet above sea level along the Metairie and Gentilly ridges—the former route of a bayou—where modern Metairie Road and City Park Avenue now run. These combined are essentially the elevations of Canal Street's 3½-mile route from the river to City Park Avenue.

The low-lying, swampy land and its bordering residential areas were once called the Back-of-Town. Some of the higher areas in the Back-of-Town, such as Bayou Road, which sits atop the Esplanade Ridge, were suitable for farms and houses as early as the eighteenth century. Faubourg St. John, which is located around modern Esplanade Avenue and Gentilly Boulevard, was subdivided in 1809 and soon had a few scattered houses. Located some distance from town, Faubourg St. John did not experience real growth until the late nineteenth and early twentieth centuries.

Similar subdivision and development did not come early to the area that evolved into outer Canal Street. Barthélémy Lafon's 1817 plan of New Orleans shows suburbs extending closely along the river from Felicity Street to Press Street. Going back from the river, the city was at most about a dozen blocks wide, and Canal Street—with its projected canal—reached only as far back as Rampart Street. Francis B. Ogden's 1829 plan of the city shows Canal Street's urban limits having grown only as far back as Basin Street. Streets appeared as far as the St. Louis Cemetery No. 2, but the area surrounding the cemetery remained virtually uninhabited. In the 1830s Canal Street was only about a mile long beyond its intersection with modern Claiborne Avenue. It simply disappeared into the woods and back swamp.

Mandina's Restaurant, on the corner of South Cortez Street and Canal in Mid-City, opened in 1898 as a corner grocery serving sandwiches. (Photo by Kerri McCaffety)

The interior of Mandina's Restaurant on Canal Street. (Photo by Kerri McCaffety)

them. In the early 1900s, this Canal Street spot was born as a combination bar room, sandwich shop, and pool hall that often hosted workers from the nearby and now-defunct American Can Company. Mandina's blossomed into an actual restaurant in 1932 when Frank and Anthony Mandina took it over from their dad, Sebastian. During World War II, the brothers fought in Europe and Anthony's wife, Miss Hilda, ran the eatery. (There's a Miss Hilda salad, a house special.) Upon the brothers' return, Anthony went back to the

The blocks of Canal Street between Rampart Street and Claiborne Avenue were well built up with some splendid townhouses—complete with impressive side bays and gardens—as early as the 1840s and 1850s. However, by the 1920s this row of mansions was being overtaken by the business district that started to expand out along Canal Street. Here, former private homes were becoming tenements and being converted into shops, while others were being torn down for new buildings and ubiquitous downtown parking lots. A few of the old houses remain, but they are only depressed shadows of their former selves.

By the 1840s streets were subdivided as far as Galvez Street, but while Canal Street was depicted as a solid line on maps, those streets crossing it beyond Claiborne Avenue were still shown only as hash marks. S. Pinestri's map of 1841 clearly identifies the built-up portion of the city, but still does not indicate any buildings past Claiborne Avenue. Several maps of the time depict a railroad track belonging to the Nashville line running along Canal Street as far as Basin Street. The railroad was never built there. Had it been constructed, the history of Canal Street would have been very different.

LAND DEALS

For a while a portion of Canal Street and some of its cross streets were owned by one of the most illustrious heroes of American history—Marie Du Motier, better known as the Marquis de la Fayette of American Revolutionary War fame. As a result of his nation's own revolution, la Fayette lost his fortune, and to assist him financially the United States Congress gave him a land grant in Louisiana in 1806.

The grant consisted of part of the City Commons surrounding New Orleans, the area that once contained forts and palisades and where Canal Street later evolved. La Fayette's grant stretched approximately as far back as modern Galvez Street, and between Tulane Avenue and Lafitte Street. Once drained, this land was recognized as important for the future development of New Orleans by municipal officials who voiced their disapproval of the proposed grant.

To the city's satisfaction, Congress agreed to New Orleans' right of ownership to the Commons, and gave it to New Orleans with the stipulation that a navigation canal be built on the Commons connecting the river to Lake Pontchartrain via Basin Street. From this act—and the never-built canal—the roots of Canal Street were laid. The Marquis de la Fayette was thus indirectly responsible for the creation of the main street of New Orleans.

The Marquis was given land further back, but still crossed part of the site of future Canal Street. The grant was essentially a triangle of real estate that stretched from Claiborne Avenue to Galvez Street and from Tulane Avenue eastward, narrowing to a point at Claiborne and Orleans avenues. La Fayette accepted the gift, and to raise money he later sold a share of it to wealthy Englishman Sir John Coghill. The latter died, and his share became the property of his nephew Sir Joshua Coghill. He in turn sold his share to New Orleanian John Hagan, who later bought out la Fayette's heirs. By the early 1830s, the property had been subdivided

by Hagan into forty-one square blocks as Faubourg Hagan, and in the early 1840s it was being sold to speculators and home seekers.

In the early 1830s beyond Faubourg Hagan there was a series of properties crossing Canal Street. Some of them were based on late eighteenth century Spanish land grants, and some were the back portions of properties fronting the upriver side of Bayou Road about a mile east of Canal Street. The bounds of the properties were predicated upon the geographical directions of both the Esplanade and Metairie ridges, with the result that the properties cut across the future route of Canal Street at oblique angles. This can still be seen today in the odd angles of several of the cemeteries near the intersection of Canal Street and City Park Avenue.

SUBDIVIDING

In the early 1830s, the area between Galvez Street and City Park Avenue was still mainly swamp land and was intersected by a number of small bayous radiating from the tip of Bayou St. John. New Orleans was a growing city, and although its main directions of growth ran parallel to the river, it was still spreading toward Lake Pontchartrain. But it grew slowly. The area past Carrollton Avenue was subdivided as part of the City of Carrollton in 1833. This section of the big Carrollton tract remained swampy and for decades served primarily agricultural purposes.

Although Canal Street's development went only to about Claiborne Avenue in the early 1840s, when Faubourg Hagan was opened, houses were soon being built as far out as Johnson Street. With additional subdivisions, Canal Street—at least on paper—reached Broad Street, and by the late 1850s it was subdivided all the way to Metairie Road. This was in spite of a report presented to the Sanitary Commission of New Orleans by Dr. E. H. Barton after the devastating 1853 yellow fever epidemic describing Canal Street beyond Broad Street as "low grounds" possessing "various open drains receiving the filth of the city."

At that time there were scattered buildings as far out as Miro Street, and by the 1870s as far as Rocheblave Street. During the next decade, urban development along Canal Street was reaching as far out as Broad Street, although for the most part Canal Street beyond Miro Street was still country living, with a few single and double cottages sprinkled among small dairies and vegetable farms serving the nearby metropolis.

HIGH WATERS

The reason for slowed development was that the section of New Orleans past Claiborne Avenue was so flood-prone. Until the beginning of the twentieth century, the city's drainage system was rudimentary at best, with a dependence on gutters and canals, which channeled water toward the Metairie Ridge and several simple paddle-wheel pumps. The pumps serving Canal Street were located on Bienville Street at Hagan Avenue, now Jefferson Davis Parkway, and were designed to drain water into Bayou St. John.

The pumps as a whole were meant to flush water over the ridge toward the lake; however, they tended to splash water around more than anything else. While they could help move water produced by a summer shower,

kitchen and Frank tended the bar until he sold his interest to his brother in the 1960s.

Today, Anthony's son Tommy is at the helm, along with daughter Cindy. He and she subscribe to the "if it ain't broke, don't fix it" theory of doing business. With the exception of adding a bit more space by expanding into the rooms of an adjacent building and installing a neon video poker machine sign that points to a discreet spot, little has changed. Mandina's still retains that increasingly elusive successful-restaurant concept—a following.

"As a child I remember going to Mandina's with the adults who wanted to drink Sazeracs after a funeral," recalls Maureen Detweiler, referring to Schoen Funeral Home across the street from the restaurant. But, of course, spending an afternoon or evening at Mandina's is more about the joy of living. There's the fried oyster po-boy served with the kind of french bread that begins to flake with crispness to the touch. Listed on the daily specials menu each Tuesday and Saturday is what many patrons would consider a quintessential corned beef and cabbage.

The tables can be filled at the height of lunch or dinnertime. If there is a wait, the time spent ordering a drink at the dark wooden bar that lines the front room of Mandina's can be spent noting who's a regular and who's new in town. For a first timer or an "all the timer," Mandina's is a Canal Street landmark that is as sturdy as the live oaks it sits under.

they were generally useless in holding back any major inundation. A heavy summer rainstorm could leave any portion of nineteenth century Canal Street, even in the business district, with standing street water.

As early as the 1830s, city authorities were trying to find ways to drain the Back-of-Town, but the difficulty with adequate drainage retarded growth. Because of flooding, New Orleans had limited land space, and by the 1870s the city was beginning to reach the limits of its habitable land. Uptown, with its wide natural levee, had the most high ground, and was the fastest-growing part of town. Downtown, with a narrow natural levee, had little available high ground, but was also filling in.

The only available direction for the city's next phase of growth was toward the lake and into an area of progressively greater flood threat. As a result, houses had already begun appearing as far back as Broad Street by the early 1880s. There were even dwellings appearing in the wilderness beyond Broad Street, even though anybody living beyond Liberty Street was considered foolish, and people living beyond Galvez Street were regarded as courting disaster.

In 1816 a crevasse at the McCarty plantation in modern Carrollton sent water as far into the city as Chartres Street in the French Quarter. In 1849 a flood from a levee break in modern River Ridge—this was the last time the city was flooded by the river—poured water past St. Charles Avenue and into the French Quarter. In both cases virtually all of Canal Street was inundated, and in 1849 some areas in the Back-of-Town were submerged under as much as nine feet of water. In both floods, water remained in some areas for months.

A view of the uptown river corner of Canal and Claiborne Avenue after an 1871 flood. At left is Stone's Infirmary. (Courtesy of The Historic New Orleans Collection)

More often, serious flooding was produced by wind-driven water off Lake Pontchartrain, and in most cases the pumps were helpless against it. One such flood occurred in 1871. A crevasse at Bonnet Carré, upriver from New Orleans, dumped water into Lake Pontchartrain, raising the lake's water level considerably. A strong north wind associated with a cold front sent lake water pouring into the swamps behind the city, and when a levee broke at Hagan Avenue, the pumps were overwhelmed.

The city was flooded as far downtown as Chartres Street. Water was knee deep on Canal Street near Claiborne Avenue and even deeper in the Broad Street area. In 1880 another lake surge sent water as far into town as Liberty Street.

Beyond Claiborne Avenue, Canal Street was initially not much more than a wide rutted path passing through woods with a few scattered houses. As a result, it was not paved in its early days. In 1859 the street was widened and leveled back from Claiborne Avenue and underbrush was removed. It was also paved with a thick layer of oyster shells as far out as Metairie Road where Canal Street reached its full length. There was a drainage canal along Canal Street past Claiborne Avenue, allowing at least this part of the street to live up to its name.

SHELL ROAD

When the Canal streetcar line was established in 1861, the track was laid over the drainage canal where the track was supported by a timber framework. There was a wood frame streetcar barn, with a tower, built on Canal at North White Street. This was later replaced by a new streetcar barn and is now the site of the Regional Transit Authority's office and transportation complex.

The Canal Street shell road became a popular route for carriage rides out into the country. By the Civil War it had become the main route to the many cemeteries and the Metairie Racetrack, which had been established near the end of the street. Unfortunately, the avenue was not always well maintained. During the bitter winter of 1880-81, New Orleans experienced a series of drenching rains along with intermittent freezes. This left the city's mostly unpaved streets in a dreadful state, with wrecked carriages and carts abandoned along many roadways.

The Canal Street shell road was especially hard hit. As it became almost impassable, funerals had to be postponed

Around 1870, when this photograph was taken, there was very little development along Canal Street below Claiborne Avenue, although by then lower Canal was a well-used shell road drive. (Courtesy of The Historic New Orleans Collection)

since hearses could not navigate the ruined shell paving and deep mud. Eight thousand barrels of shells were required to make the street passable again, but even with that, little was done to maintain the important artery. In 1888 *The Mascot,* a local commentary and scandal sheet, described the Canal Street shell road as "a hog-wallow prairie," consisting of "hills and hollows." It was not unheard of for hearses on the way to one of the cemeteries to tip over among the muddy "hills and hollows."

Ironically, as early as 1884 electric streetlights illuminated Canal Street as far out as the cemeteries. This was one of the most impressive street lighting projects of the day, especially since from Broad Street to Metairie Road the lights went through virtually open country along a poorly paved road.

GOING MODERN

Modern systems for providing drinking water, sewage disposal, and drainage were slow to develop in New Orleans. In 1899 that changed. After years of struggle on the part of health officials and business groups, the city's voters finally approved a bond issue for new improvements that almost overnight lifted New Orleans from the dark ages of municipal services into the twentieth century. The drainage system finally allowed New Orleanians to move without anxiety into low-lying neighborhoods, including Mid-City and outer Canal Street. Although Mid-City and Canal Street beyond Broad Street had been subdivided for years, few houses had been built in the section before the twentieth century. With the new drainage system building activity increased appreciably.

Even before improved drainage, some large buildings appeared in the countrified confines of outer Canal Street in the nineteenth century. In 1839 the Maison de Santé, Dr. Warren Stone's Infirmary, was built at the uptown river corner of Canal Street and Claiborne Avenue. At the time it was on the fringes of town. Dr. Stone's Infirmary was an elegant, temple-like Greek Revival structure surrounded by gardens. It operated as a hospital until 1867, but had been demolished by the early 1880s when the lot was used as a wood yard. Since the 1960s a hotel has occupied the site.

Across Canal Street from Dr. Stone's Infirmary was a large cotton press that covered two square blocks. Built in the early 1840s as Collin's Cotton Press, it was later better known as Wood's Cotton Press. It was demolished and replaced in the 1890s by the ornate Crescent Brewery. The brewery was converted into a candy factory during Prohibition in the 1920s, and a portion of the building ended its days in the 1950s housing the automobile dealership of O. E. Haring. During the 1920s and 1930s, the building shared the block with the Coca Cola Bottling Company.

In the early 1960s, when this section of Canal Street was evolving into an area of office buildings, a pair of slab-like skyscrapers was planned for the site, but they were never built. Office development was shifting to the newly widened Poydras Street.

HEAVY RAIN

In 1915 an unnamed hurricane tore into the city with 120 M.P.H. wind gusts (170 M.P.H. gusts at Boothville, near the mouth of the river),

Wood's Cotton Press circa 1870. It stood at the river corner of Canal and North Claiborne between the 1850s and 1890s. (Courtesy of The Historic New Orleans Collection)

O. E. Haring's automobile dealership stood on this river corner of Canal and North Claiborne in 1950, and its offices were housed in what was once part of the Crescent Brewery. Wood's Cotton Press was also here at one time. (Courtesy of The Historic New Orleans Collection)

and produced considerable street flooding throughout the city. Especially hard hit were sections of Canal Street, Mid-City, and other low-lying neighborhoods. Heavy rain was the culprit, since flooding from Lake Pontchartrain in the built-up part of the city was not as serious as some had expected, except along the lakefront at West End and Bucktown, where people had to be rescued. Canal Street lay under several feet of water, much to the enjoyment of children but to the irritation of adults fortunate enough to own automobiles.

The storm also helped bring down Crescent Row, an ancient Canal Street landmark dating from about 1850 between North Roman and North Prieur streets. This was a block-long series of attached wooden townhouses built with a common facade adorned by a row of numerous wooden columns. These townhouses were among the very earliest buildings constructed on Canal Street past Claiborne Avenue, but by 1915 were nothing more than a down-at-the-heels tenement nicknamed Bed Bug Row. It was so extensively damaged by the hurricane that it was unceremoniously pulled down.

In 2005 the Canal Street area once again experienced flooding—this time as part of the worst natural disaster in the history of the United

South Claiborne Avenue, looking toward the corner of Canal, photographed by Jay Dearborn Edwards in the late 1850s. The residential character of the neighborhood is apparent. (Courtesy of The Historic New Orleans Collection)

States. Hurricane Katrina swept through the city, unleashing unprecedented devastation. A break in the 17th Street Canal caused the waters of Lake Pontchartrain to pour through the streets. In many areas, up to six feet of water was reported.

HIGHER EDUCATION

One of the most historically important educational facilities on outer Canal Street was Straight University, located between South Tonti and South Rocheblave streets. Straight University was established for black students in 1869. Its first home was on Esplanade Avenue at Bourbon Street. Then, following a fire in 1877, the school moved into new and larger quarters on Canal Street. The university operated in a series of sprawling frame buildings until 1935 when it became part of Dillard University and moved to Gentilly Boulevard.

For a few years after that, the old frame Victorian buildings of Straight University served as a school and YWCA for blacks, but in 1950 the complex was torn down and replaced by the handsome, modern headquarters of Pan American Life Insurance Company. With the appearance of numerous low-rise office buildings, Canal Street between Claiborne Avenue and Broad Street was becoming an extension of the business district.

Richardson Memorial Hall, another important Canal Street educational facility, was located between North Robertson and North Villere streets. Built in the 1890s, this building served as Tulane University's School of Medicine. The massive structure was set back from the street on property that encompassed half a square block. In 1908 a new medical school was constructed on the Tulane campus, and the Canal Street building was demolished before it was forty years old. Much of the site was converted into a parking lot.

Some grand homes were being built on late nineteenth century Canal Street. The home owned by Charles A. Orleans is still standing. Orleans was one of the most successful builders of cemetery monuments in New Orleans, and his elaborately ornamented home was located on Canal Street at the corner of South Derbigny Street. Built in 1889, it was one of the grand mansions of New Orleans. It boasted an array of cupolas, gables, balconies, and gingerbread, combining the influence of Queen Anne and Eastlake, both highly popular Victorian architectural styles. The house was built in a quiet residential neighborhood, but it was still only a few blocks from the business district.

Another lavish Victorian house with its gables and cupolas was built for V. J. Virgin at the corner of North Scott Street. Virgin owned a successful nursery and florist business, and was associated with Reuter's Seed Company. His house was even more flamboyant than the Charles Orleans house. It was on a property that covered nearly a city block and had a lush garden surrounded by a low stone wall. Typical of the Queen Anne style, it was one of the most spectacular houses in New Orleans, and featured conical roofs and a tall belvedere. The house, now minus some of its nineteenth century ornamentation but still surrounded by lawns and gardens, has long been the headquarters of Jacob Schoen & Son, Inc. Funeral Home.

When built in the early 1950s, the Pan American Life Insurance Building in the 2700 block of Canal was one of New Orleans' prime examples of post-Modern architecture. The company relocated to Poydras Street in the 1980s. (Courtesy of The Historic New Orleans Collection)

The Tulane Medical School in the late 1890s. The school operated out of this building until 1908. The structure was demolished in the late 1930s. (Courtesy of The Historic New Orleans Collection)

This structure, one of the elegant houses of the 1880s on Canal Street, was built by Charles A. Orleans. Although it has lost some of its ornamentation, it is still used as an office building. (Courtesy of The Historic New Orleans Collection)

The V. J. Virgin house was one of the finest residences on late nineteenth century Canal Street. Although altered, it is still in use as the Schoen Funeral Home.

The entrance of the V.J. Virgin house, modified into a somewhat Spanish Mission style, in the 1930s.

The entrance hall of Schoen Funeral Home, which has occupied the former residence
of V. J. Virgin since the late 1930s. (Photo by Peggy Scott Laborde)

A carved angel in the marble mantel that was part of the early 1900s V. J. Virgin house. (Photo by Peggy Scott Laborde)

The Canal streetcar framed by one of the arches of the Schoen Funeral Home. (Courtesy of Peggy Scott Laborde)

When V. J. Virgin moved into his fashionable new home, it was situated in an idyllic country setting of farms and a few scattered houses—all only about three miles from the heart of downtown New Orleans. However, this changed rapidly as the twentieth century dawned. The city's new drainage system opened Canal Street and the whole Back-of-Town to rapid urbanization, within two decades turning farms into suburbs all the way back to City Park Avenue.

While some of the big houses such as those owned by Charles Orleans and V. J. Virgin would have comfortably fit along any upscale residential street in the nation, including New Orleans' own St. Charles Avenue, the houses that were invading the grassy lands of Canal Street were generally not grand. Nevertheless, they were comfortable and in keeping with the solidly middle-class families that were moving there.

Beyond Broad Street, there were rows of mostly single houses. Some were raised—even over garages, to welcome the coming of the automobile

Magdalena Holzer, widow of an ironworks owner, built this home in 1912. Featuring fine architectural detail and stained glass, it was restored in 2000 and today is the Block-Keller House, a bed and breakfast. (Photo by Peggy Scott Laborde)

An example of the fine craftsmanship of early twentieth century homes in the residential section of Canal Street.

The late Thomas Griffin was a well-known New Orleans newspaper columnist. When he was young, his family lived in this house at the corner of Canal and Hennessey streets, shown circa 1910. (Courtesy of The Historic New Orleans Collection)

age. They were not nearly as ornamented as houses of earlier decades. Still, they were representative of the tastes and styles of the 1910s and the Roaring Twenties and included bungalows and Spanish Revival architecture. While single- and double-shotgun houses had been the hallmark of older sections of New Orleans, this was not the case along Canal Street as twentieth century floor plans proliferated.

With the incursion of commercial establishments, some of the larger residences have been lost. The remaining ones are being turned into law offices. A bright yellow Ronald McDonald House is an asset to the street, and bed and breakfast activity has caused some structures to be restored.

SCHOOLS AND CHURCHES

As Canal Street grew, it became a neighborhood of families with children, and with children came the need for schools. Prior to 1900 there were few schools on or near Canal Street, especially in the stretches beyond Broad Street. Soon after the arrival of the new century and population spiraled upward, new public schools began to appear in the Canal Street corridor. This growth in schools coincided not only with surging populations, but with the City Beautiful movement and a growing awareness of the importance of at least a high school education.

As the Mid-City neighborhood grew, the Mid-City Library was built on Canal Street. The structure is now used as commercial space. (Courtesy of the New Orleans Public Library)

The interior of the Mid-City Library, which is no longer in use. (Courtesy of the New Orleans Public Library)

Today's St. Anthony of Padua Roman Catholic Church was built in 1923 following the founding of the parish eight years earlier. The attractive facade is designed in the Spanish Mission style.

The current Sacred Heart of Jesus Church was built in 1924, even though the parish was founded in 1879. Two earlier churches attested to the rapid growth of the Mid-City area along Canal Street. Jazz great Louis Armstrong was baptized in this parish in 1901.

New public schools at the time were usually housed in large and architecturally impressive buildings. Typical of this period is New Orleans Boys High School, built on Canal at North White Street in 1912. This was one of many schools constructed in New Orleans between 1910 and World War II and has been known in the more recent past as Warren Easton High School.

Our Lady of the Sacred Heart of Jesus Roman Catholic Church, which once operated a school, was a popular place for high school dances. A musical history note: jazz great Louis Armstrong was baptized in an earlier church structure on the site of today's house of worship. Architecturally distinctive on this street of churches is St. Anthony of Padua Roman Catholic Church, a Spanish Mission-style structure only a few blocks from the end of Canal Street near the cemeteries.

MONUMENTS

From the 1870s into the early twentieth century, many monuments dedicated to heroes of the Confederacy were constructed around New Orleans. Two such monuments face each other across Canal Street at Jefferson Davis Parkway, formerly Hagan Avenue. This is one of the few streets in New Orleans wider than Canal Street. One of the monuments is a statue of Confederate President Jefferson Davis showing him standing, arm lifted, addressing the people. The monument was dedicated in 1911, fifty years after Davis was sworn in as president of the Confederacy.

Across Canal Street from the Jefferson Davis Monument is a smaller monument dedicated to Col. Charles Didier Dreux, the first Louisiana officer to volunteer for service in the Civil War and also the first one to be killed. The monument, which consists of a bust of Dreux atop a pedestal, was dedicated in 1922.

GETTING THEIR MAN

On May 1, 1936, the quiet Mid-City neighborhood became the center of national attention. Bearing the not very flattering nickname of "Old Creepy," Alvin Karpis, a member of the notorious Barker-Karpis Gang, was arrested. He was wanted for kidnapping, murder, and robbery. Karpis had rented an apartment on Canal Street, and twelve federal agents, accompanied by none other than FBI Director J. Edgar Hoover, confronted him. He was taken without a shot being fired. It was the only arrest ever made personally by Hoover. Karpis spent twenty-six years in Alcatraz, served time elsewhere, and was finally freed in 1969. He died ten years later. The house he lived in on Canal Street was the site of a Walgreens drug store.

THE RESTAURANT NEIGHBORHOOD

Canal Street beyond downtown has had its share of restaurants and lounges. Near Broad Street is the popular Betsy's Pancake House. The building formerly housed Musso's a favorite stop for a nightcap after an evening downtown. New Orleans jazz pianist Armand Hug performed

The Jefferson Davis Monument, which still stands, was erected in 1912 on Hagan Avenue, which was renamed Jefferson Davis Parkway and rivals Canal Street in width. (Courtesy of The Historic New Orleans Collection)

there on a regular basis. Another popular stop was the Swamp Room, closer to Carrollton Avenue and known for its giant wooden alligator in the middle of the dance floor.

During the 1960s at North Broad Street and Canal was an A&G Cafeteria, where organist Ray McNamara played for customers. A Rite-Aid drug store now occupies the site. Mandina's, a restaurant featuring Creole cooking with an Italian influence, remains a popular dining spot for both locals and visitors.

Near the corner of Canal and Carrollton Avenue have been almost twenty restaurants. Leading to even more restaurants down North Carrollton is the Canal streetcar spur, a turn-off on the line that extends to City Park. Close to the cemeteries is the Beach Corner, a 24-hour bar and grill.

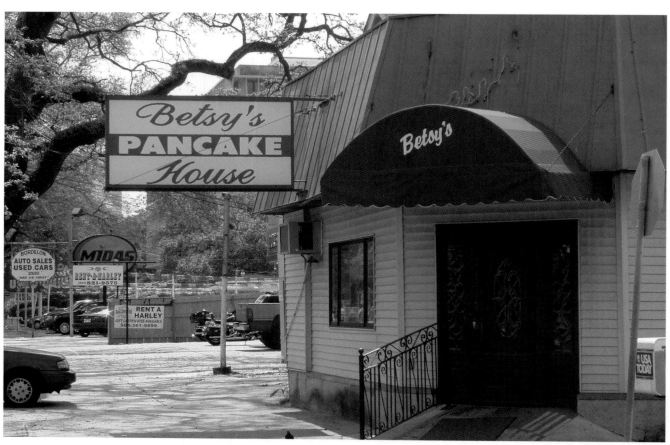

Betsy's Pancake House on Canal Street in Mid-City was once Musso's Lounge, a popular spot for a nightcap after an evening downtown.

MUSSO'S
Restaurant and Lounge

HARRY BUISSON
PHIL. HEISLER
Proprietors

524-0721
2542 CANAL STREET
at Dorgenois

— PIANO BAR —

Musso's Lounge was one of New Orleans' most popular lounges. Pianist Armand Hug played there for many years. (Courtesy of Bob Murret)

Decorated with hanging moss, the Swamp Room was known for its live music acts and a dance floor called the "lagoon," which had a stuffed imitation alligator in the center. (Courtesy of Bob Murret)

Mid-City's emergence as a neighborhood of eateries is one more amenity of an old neighborhood experiencing new vitality. While commercial use dominates most of Canal Street in Mid-City, the hope for the neighborhood is that the older buildings that have survived will be preserved to reflect the early growth of New Orleans' "main street."

TODAY

In 1993 the Mid-City neighborhood was designated an "Historic District" by the National Register of Historic Places, acknowledging that the architecture of the area is not only historically significant but also reflects the culture of the community. While the designation offers little protection from demolition of older structures along Canal Street, it is an important first step.

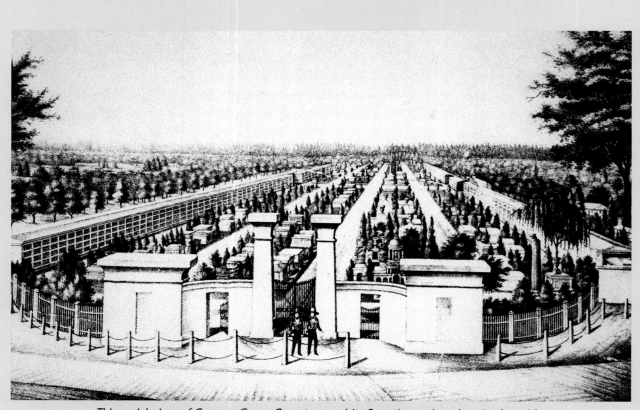

This aerial view of Cypress Grove Cemetery and its Egyptian-style pylons in the mid-nineteenth century shows how countrified its surroundings were at the time. (Courtesy of The Historic New Orleans Collection)

CHAPTER FIFTEEN
Down to the Cemeteries

METAIRIE ROAD—RENAMED City Park Avenue in the early twentieth century east of the New Basin Canal (Pontchartrain Expressway)—is located on relatively high ground on the Metairie Ridge, which is about three feet above sea level. There were farms along its route from the early days of New Orleans. Once considered far from the center of town, it began evolving in the 1830s into one of the most important sections of the city's life—and perhaps more correctly, death.

In 1838 the Metairie Racetrack was established on Metairie Road a short distance above its intersection with Canal Street on the site of today's Metairie Cemetery. A few years later it was joined by the Oak Land Race Course across Metairie Road where the New Orleans Country Club is today. In 1853 the Metairie Jockey Club began managing the Metairie track, which had become one of the outstanding racing venues in the United States.

When the Metairie Racetrack opened, it could be reached via the New Basin Canal shell road—today's route of the Pontchartrain Expressway—either by omnibus or by the train that ran along Jackson Avenue and the canal. A popular stopping-off place for refreshments was the Half Way House on the canal at Metairie Road. The Metairie Racetrack was not on Canal Street, but it became part of Canal Street's world, especially after the establishment of the Canal streetcar line in 1861 when Canal Street became one of the primary routes for going to the races.

Often a monument or some other feature is located at the end of a great boulevard. This is true in a sense of Canal Street, but instead of a single monument proclaiming the end of the street, one finds a multitude of monuments. Beginning in the early 1840s, a cluster of cemeteries grew at the point where Canal Street rather ignominiously faded into the woods and swamps.

The first of the cemeteries to be established was Cypress Grove—the Firemen's Cemetery. It was founded in 1840 by the Firemen's Charitable and Benevolent Association, and in 1841 it accepted its first remains, that of Irad Ferry, a volunteer fireman who died in the line of duty. His monument stands near the cemetery's entrance.

The entrance to the cemetery is embellished by distinctive and elegant pylons and lodges designed in the Egyptian style. Cypress Grove became a popular cemetery among the city's Protestant families. The Girod Street

BOTTINELLI PLACE

Located between Chevra Thilim and St. Patrick's cemeteries is a triangular block of buildings with a short cul-de-sac called Bottinelli Place. Originally South Anthony Street, it was rededicated in December 1975 in honor of Theodoro Francisco Bottinelli who arrived in New Orleans from his native Italy around 1906 as a young man and became one of New Orleans' most noted sculptors.

Among his works is the baptismal font at St. Anthony of Padua Roman Catholic Church at 4640 Canal Street, just a few blocks from Bottinelli Place. But his great specialty was carving eagles. Examples of his eagles may be found alongside his carved Corinthian capitals at the Whitney National Bank Building at St. Charles and Gravier streets, the towering United States Custom House in Boston (now a Marriott Hotel), and along the bridge crossing the Potomac River between Washington, D.C. and Arlington, Virginia. One of his largest works is not an eagle, but the representation of Robert E. Lee on his horse, Traveler, at the Confederate Memorial at Stone Mountain, Georgia.

209

Theodoro Francisco Bottinelli's son, the late Theodore Bottinelli, was instrumental in having the street renamed in honor of his father. At about the same time, the younger Bottinelli began to accumulate architectural elements from demolished buildings and installed them on buildings at Bottinelli Place. His first acquisition—as well as the most obvious detail visible

Bottinelli Place is nestled between several Jewish cemeteries and St. Patrick's Cemetery. (Photo by Peggy Scott Laborde)

The two towers crowning Bottinelli Place were salvaged from Temple Sinai Synagogue, which stood on Carondelet Street near Howard Avenue from about 1880 until it was demolished in 1977.

The pylons and lodges of Cypress Grove have hardly changed from the way they appeared in the mid-nineteenth century.

A religious mosaic on the Cypress Grove Cemetery wall facing Canal Street.

from Canal Street—are the crowning twin towers of Temple Sinai. This Jewish synagogue was a landmark on Carondelet Street near Howard Avenue from the 1870s until its demolition in 1977.

In addition to the towers, there is also a series of cast-iron columns from the interior of the temple that now forms part of the exterior ornamentation. In 1977 quartz was imported from Italy and used as cobbles to pave the street.

On a neighboring building, one may see adornments that include the mansard roof, windows, and tile frames from an elegant Victorian mansion. It had once been the archbishops' residence not far from the site of St. Aloysius High School on Esplanade Avenue near St. Claude. On yet another building, there is a railing replica of the ironwork on the Pontalba Buildings on Jackson Square.

Theodoro Francisco Bottinelli died in 1932, and in 1936 his widow, Emma, opened Quality Florist at 4900 Canal. It operated until 1998. Next to the former Quality Florist building is a red tile driveway. At its sidewalk end on Canal Street is a massive ironwork canopy. Created by Lorio Ironworks, the canopy was a backdrop to the throne used by the delegate of Pope Pius XI at the Eucharistic Congress of 1938 at a Mass in City Park. On either side of the backdrop are the Gothic wings of the throne. Also preserved is a cast-iron design of grape leaves that had been used to support the canopy.

Following the Eucharistic Congress, Lorio's was able to

recover these parts, and in the late 1970s presented them to Theodore Bottinelli. With the addition of the initial B at the top of the ironwork, this became part of an architectural treasure trove not far from the end of Canal Street.

Cemetery, the city's first Protestant place of interment (straddling parts of today's New Orleans Centre shopping mall and the nearby Louisiana Superdome parking garage), began a slow decline, was abandoned, and finally was razed in 1957. The cemetery's remains were moved to Odd Fellows Rest.

In 1841 the Irish congregation of St. Patrick's Catholic Church on Camp Street opened St. Patrick's Cemetery One, Two, Three, and Four. This cemetery crosses Canal Street and City Park Avenue, thus its division into four parts. It occupies land the church purchased from a free man of color. When City Park Avenue was widened in 1909, a portion of St. Patrick's Three was acquired for part of the paving project.

In 1846 the Jewish congregation Nefuzoth Yehudah established a cemetery on outer Canal Street in the modern 4900 block and called it the Dispersed of Judah. The benefactor of this congregation was Judah Touro, and there is a plaque honoring him. Ultimately, the congregation also gave their synagogue his name. It is fitting that the cemetery is on Canal Street, since Touro was an important Canal Street developer, and when he died in 1854, he left funds to beautify the business portion of the street. After Touro's death, the city council renamed Canal Street in his honor, but the popularity of the long-established designation soon prompted the council to restore it.

In the 4800 block of Canal Street is the Temmeme Derech Cemetery, which was founded in 1858 and renamed the Gates of Prayer in 1939 when that congregation absorbed it. In the same block are two other Jewish cemeteries, Chevra Thilim, taken over by the Gates of Prayer in 1950, and Beth Israel.

The gates to the Odd Fellows Cemetery.

In 1847 the Independent Order of Odd Fellows obtained a pie-shaped piece of land next to St. Patrick's Cemetery at the corner of Canal Street and Metairie Road. In 1849 Odd Fellows Cemetery was dedicated with a great procession that revealed the difficulty of using an unpaved Canal Street to travel to the cemeteries. The parade, with circus bandwagons and an elaborate funeral car, passed over many of the city's most important streets but had to take a detour to the cemetery via the New Basin Canal shell road.

Another 1847 cemetery is owned by Charity Hospital. It is laid out between Cypress Grove and St. Patrick's cemeteries. This is a potter's field dedicated to receiving the bodies of indigents who died at Charity Hospital. Many of those interred there succumbed to yellow fever in the nineteenth century.

In response to the popular acceptance of Cypress Grove Cemetery, in 1852 the Firemen's Charitable and Benevolent Association opened

The Odd Fellows Cemetery is lined with wall vaults.

Tombs from the nineteenth century in St. Patrick's No. 1 Cemetery at the end of Canal Street.

Detail of the Gothic Revival Firemen's Monument in Greenwood Cemetery. The monument was erected in 1887 by Charles Orleans, whose house was on Canal Street. (Courtesy of The Historic New Orleans Collection)

A silhouette of the Gothic Revival Firemen's Monument by noted sculptor Alexander Doyle.

An elk stands proudly atop the grassy mound tomb of Lodge Number 30 of the Benevolent Protective Order of Elks. This monument was completed in 1912 and is near the entrance of Greenwood Cemetery.

Greenwood Cemetery. Several large monuments can be found there, including a Confederate monument. Dedicated in 1874, it was the first Civil War monument erected in New Orleans. Also at Greenwood, at the corner of Canal Street and City Park Avenue, is the Gothic Revival Firemen's Monument, with its figure of a volunteer fireman. Across from it is the tomb for Lodge 30 of the Benevolent Order of the Elks, a grassy mound topped by the figure of an elk.

Following the Civil War, financial problems prompted the dissolution of the Metairie Jockey Club and the eventual closure of the Metairie Racetrack. In 1872 the Louisiana Jockey Club was formed, and the racetrack operations were relocated to the Creole Race Course, now the Fair Grounds. The old Metairie track was sold to a group of businessmen who converted the site into one of the most notable cemeteries in the United States. The first burial in the new Metairie Cemetery took place in 1873.

The cemetery's road system was designed around the oval of the old race course, and its general pattern was based upon the large and spacious rural cemeteries common in the northeast. The impressive monument to the Army of Tennessee, an equestrian statue of Gen. Albert

The Metairie Cemetery in the mid-1890s. When it opened in the early 1870s, it was designed in the manner of the park-like cemeteries in the northeast United States, rather than the crowded, wall-enclosed cemeteries in the older sections of New Orleans. (Courtesy of The Historic New Orleans Collection)

Hope Mausoleum is also part of the Canal Street section of cemeteries.

Sidney Johnston atop a grassy mound, was erected in the cemetery in 1887.

Though not buried there, another Confederate general with a presence in the Metairie Cemetery is Stonewall Jackson, whose statue stands atop the column of the monument to the Army of Northern Virginia dedicated in 1881. When Confederate President Jefferson Davis died in New Orleans in 1889, he was buried in the tomb of the Army of Northern Virginia, although his remains were removed to Richmond, Virginia, in 1893. The entrance to the Metairie Cemetery dates only to 1961, since its original gate was destroyed for the construction of an overpass.

Until the early twentieth century, the land beyond the intersection of Canal Street and Metairie Road was open country shrouded by dense swamp, tangled undergrowth, grasses, and weeds that stretched with little interruption to the shores of Lake Pontchartrain. It was an area where a person could still hear a myriad of insect and bird noises and even the roars of alligators. This changed soon after the start of the twentieth century.

A new red streetcar glides past the cemeteries end of Canal Street, the end of the line.

Lakeview was subdivided in 1907, although it would be years before it was heavily built up. In 1911 Canal Boulevard, picking up where Canal Street ended, gave locals another route to the lake besides the shell road along the New Basin Canal. From this "extension" of Canal Street came the birth of the troublesome dogleg intersection at the cemeteries' junction with Canal Street and City Park Avenue. It also allowed New Orleanians to reach the lake directly via Canal Street.

Today, it is not unusual to see tourists getting off at the end of the line to tour the cemeteries—a reminder that these Cities of the Dead continue to be appreciated by the living.

CHAPTER SIXTEEN
Hurricane Katrina

On Monday, August 29, 2005, downtown Canal Street, once known for its lavish movie theatres, became the setting of a horror show called Hurricane Katrina.

Some Canal Street stores were looted. The greater problem, however, was the water. A break in the 17th Street Canal levee five miles away affected a major part of the city, a city that thought it had escaped major damage from what was believed to be a Category Five hurricane.

The river end of Canal Street remained dry since the Mississippi River levee did not overflow its banks. The flooding came from the opposite direction. The 17th Street Canal normally empties into Lake Pontchartrain. The break (one of three from the lake) flooded much of the

Canal Street on Monday, August 29, 2005, 3:00 P.M. Katrina has already passed over New Orleans but the street has not flooded yet. (Courtesy of Neil Alexander)

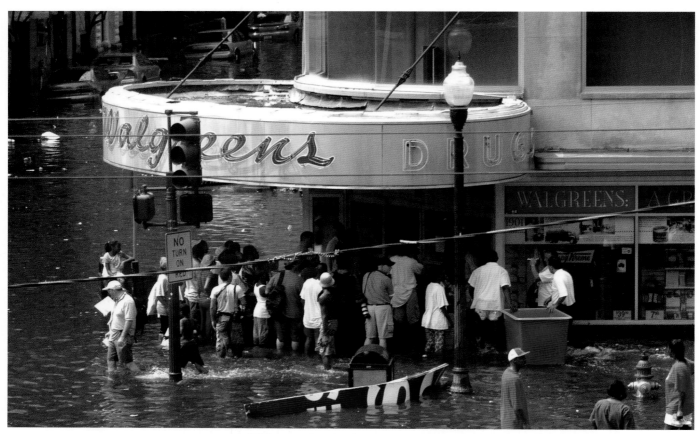

Walgreens flooded following Hurricane Katrina. (Courtesy of Cheryl Gerber)

Tourists from the Ritz-Carlton view the damage following Hurricane Katrina. (Courtesy of Cheryl Gerber)

Looking down Bourbon Street on Wednesday, August 31, 2005, toward Canal Street. Floodwaters reach all the way to Bourbon Street and looters set fire to some shops on Canal Street, bringing out the fire department. (Courtesy of Neil Alexander)

Looting activity on Canal Street following Hurricane Katrina. (Courtesy of Cheryl Gerber)

city from the lake to the river, including parts of Canal Steet's residential and business districts.

John Hill, Baton Rouge bureau chief for Gannett Newspapers, recalls his first look at Canal Street a few days after Katrina hit:

> From that first jarring sight of a denuded Canal Street, there was a long arc during which every available inch filled up with television satellite trucks, RVs, then Red Cross and Salvation Army trucks, cars double-parked, then they slowly pulled away. I kept thinking how isolated they were from the action. At night, since there was no electricity, all you could see on the street were the lights provided by generators in the vehicles. It was very eerie; it chilled me to the bone.

Hill continues:

> There was a Salvation Army crisis counseling center on the street. I remember folks waiting in line there for food. The other thing that struck me was how solemn people were, and at the same time, the extraordinary kindness they showed to each other. Canal Street has never seemed so human and so gracious to me. "The kindness of strangers" took on a very different meaning. Here and there, there were broken windows, but the strong military presence everywhere made me feel safer than I ever have before.

The foot of Canal Street on September 7, 2005. Military vehicles are seen parked by the Aquarium of the Americas. (Courtesy of Neil Alexander)

According to Hill, "It was months, really the weekend of January 21 [2006], before Canal looked normal to me again."

After the flooding, the Great Wide Way truly resembled a canal.

Boats rescuing residents were a common sight. The Canal streetcar barn flooded, damaging locally built streetcars that were only a little over a year old. Many homes, churches, and businesses were devastated. Mid-City was suddenly once again a swamp.

Fortunately, the estimate of six months needed to drain the floodwaters from New Orleans turned out to be inaccurate. In a matter of weeks, the city was dry. Gradually, Canal Street returned to life as a functioning thoroughfare. For all of its history, though, Canal Street never faced as bumpy a road as it did after Katrina.

The authors would like to acknowledge the generous assistance of The Historic New Orleans Collection in providing many of the images in this book.

THE COLLECTION
THE HISTORIC NEW ORLEANS COLLECTION
533 Royal Street • 70130-2179 • www.hnoc.org • (504) 523-4662

The Historic New Orleans Collection is a privately endowed museum and research center located in the heart of the French Quarter. It was established in 1966 by Gen. and Mrs. L. Kemper Williams, avid collectors of materials related to Louisiana history and culture.

Located inside a complex of historic buildings at 533 Royal Street are the Williams Gallery, where changing exhibitions are available to the public at no charge, ten permanent exhibition galleries devoted to illustrating the history of the city, state, and Gulf South where docent guided tours are available at a modest fee, the historic house residence of General and Mrs. Williams, and a museum shop. This is one of the most significant groups of buildings in New Orleans and includes the Merieult House, which is The Collection's main entrance on Royal Street. Dating from 1792, the Merieult House survived the great fire of 1794, making it one of the oldest buildings in New Orleans.

A more recent addition to The Historic New Orleans Collection is the Williams Research Center, at 410 Chartres Street. It is in a former police station and jail built in 1915, and following extensive renovation by The Collection was opened to the public in 1996.

The Collection's research center had originally been located in three separate reading rooms at the Royal Street complex serving the library, manuscripts, and pictorial divisions. The Williams Research Center allowed the reading rooms to merge, thus providing greater availability of materials and convenience to both patrons and staff. The Williams Research Center is open at no charge to anyone interested in studying New Orleans and Louisiana, and while shelves are closed to browsers, staff is available to assist with The Collection's extensive holdings of manuscripts, books, and images.

Bibliography

Bacot, H. Parrott, Barbara SoRelle Bacot, Sally Kittredge Reeves, John Magill, and John H. Lawrence. *Marie Adrien Persac: Louisiana Artist.* Baton Rouge: Louisiana State University Press, 2000.

Behrman, Martin. *New Orleans: A History of Three Public Utilities: Sewerage, Water and Drainage, and Their Influence upon the Health and Progress of a Big City.* New Orleans: Brandao Print, 1914.

Casey, Powell A. *Encyclopedia of Forts, Posts, Named Camps and Other Military Installations in Louisiana 1700-1981.* Baton Rouge: Claitor's, 1983.

Chase, John. *Frenchmen, Desire, Good Children . . . And Other Streets of New Orleans!* New Orleans: Crager, 1949. Reprint, Gretna, La.: Pelican, 2001.

Christovich, Mary Louise, ed., Roulhac Toledano, Betsy Swanson, and Pat Holden, with essays by Samuel Wilson, Jr. and Bernard Lemann. *New Orleans Architecture Volume II: The American Secto*r (Faubourg St. Mary). Gretna, La.: Pelican, 1972.

Christovich, Mary Louise, ed., Leonard V. Huber, Peggy McDowell, and Mary Louise Christovich. *New Orleans Architecture Volume III: The Cemeteries.* Gretna, La.: Pelican, 1974.

Clement, William E. *Over a Half-Century of Electricity and Gas Industry Development in New Orleans.* New Orleans: New Orleans Public Service, Inc., 1947.

Cruise, Boyd. History cards under various subject headings, housed in The Historic New Orleans Collection.

Dabney, Thomas Ewing. *Historic Holmes: The Growth of a Great Business Institution and a Great City.* New Orleans: D. H. Holmes Co., 1925.

Engelhardt, George W., pub. *The City of New Orleans: The Book of the Chamber of Commerce and Industry of Louisiana.* New Orleans: George W. Engelhardt, 1894.

Federal Writer's Project, Works Project Administration. *New Orleans City Guide.* Boston: Houghton Mifflin, 1938.

Hendrickson, Robert. *The Grand Emporiums: The Illustrated History of America's Great Department Stores.* New York: Stein and Day, 1979.

Hennick, Louis C. and E. Harper Charlton. *The Streetcars of New Orleans.* Gretna, La.: Pelican, 1975.

Huber, Leonard V., with introduction by Samuel Wilson, Jr. *Landmarks of New Orleans.* New Orleans: Louisiana Landmarks Society and Orleans Parish Landmarks Commission, 1984.

Huber, Leonard V. *Mardi Gras: A Pictorial History of Carnival in New Orleans.* Gretna, La.: Pelican, 1977.

Huber, Leonard V. *New Orleans: A Pictorial History.* New York: Crown, 1980 edition.

Insurance Maps of New Orleans Louisiana, vols. 1 and 2. New York: Sanborn-Perris Map Co., 1896.

Insurance Maps of New Orleans Louisiana, vols. 2 and 3. New York: Sanborn Map Co., 1908.

Insurance Maps of New Orleans Louisiana, vols. 2 and 3. New York: Sanborn Map Co., 1908 corrected to 1939.

Jewell, Edward, ed. *Jewell's Crescent City Illustrated.* New Orleans, 1873.

Kemp, John R. *New Orleans: An Illustrated History.* Woodland Hills, Calif.: Windsor, 1981.

Kemp, John R. and Linda Orr King, eds. *Louisiana Images 1880-1920: A Photographic Essay by Georges François Mugnier.* Baton Rouge: Louisiana State University Press, 1975.

Laborde, Peggy Scott. "Canal Street: The Great Wide Way." WYES-TV, Greater New Orleans Educational Television Foundation, 1992.

Laborde, Peggy Scott. "Satchmo's River Days," from "Reading the River." PBS, 1992.

Laborde, Peggy Scott. "Where New Orleans Shopped." WYES-TV, Greater New Orleans Educational Television Foundation, 2002.

Lafon, Barthélémy. "Plan of the City and Environs of New Orleans, Taken from actual Survey." Baltimore, MD, 1816, a map housed in The Historic New Orleans Collection, 1945.3.

Leach, William. *Land of Dreams: Merchants, Power, and the Rise of a New American Culture.* New York: Pantheon, 1993.

Lewis, Peirce. *New Orleans: The Making of an Urban Landscape.* Cambridge, Mass.: Ballinger, 1976.

McCaffety, Kerri. *Etouffee Mon Amour: The Great Restaurants of New Orleans.* Gretna, La.: Pelican, 2002.

Magill, John. "A Brief History of New Orleans Hotels and Restaurants." *New Orleans Preservation in Print,* October 1987.

Magill, John. "Canal Street is 150 Years Old." *New Orleans Preservation in Print,* December 1985.

Magill, John. "Canal Street's Glamorous History." *New Orleans Preservation in Print,* December 1988.

Magill, John. "The curtain rose, then fell on . . . The Theaters of New Orleans," *New Orleans Preservation in Print,* May 1988.

Magill, John. "1872: New Orleans and the time of the first Rex Parade." *New Orleans Magazine,* January 1997.

Magill, John. "The Environment of Mardi Gras." *Gambit,* February 11, 1986.

Magill, John. "From Plantations to Office Towers." *New Orleans Magazine,* June 1995.

Magill, John. "From the levee to the swamp: The Evolution of Downtown." *New Orleans Magazine,* June 2000, 58-63.

Magill, John. "Gone with the flow: Vignettes from riverfront history." *New Orleans Magazine,* June 2002.

Magill, John. "Street Smarts: Canal a History." *New Orleans Magazine,* June 1998.

Magill, John T. "New Orleans Through Three Centuries," from *Charting Louisiana: Five Hundred Years of Maps,* Alfred E. Lemmon, John T. Magill, and Jason R. Wiese, eds., New Orleans: The Historic New Orleans Collection, 2003.

Magill, John Tylden. "Municipal Improvements in New Orleans in the 1880s." Master's thesis, Louisiana State University in New Orleans, 1972.

Magill, John, Mary Lou Eichhorn, and Mark Cave. "In a New Light." *Louisiana Cultural Vistas,* Winter 1999-2000.

New Orleans Louisiana Volume Two. New York: Sanborn Map Publishing Co., 1885.

New Orleans Times-Picayune.

Ogden, Francis B. "Plan of the City of New-Orleans." New York, 1829, a map housed in The Historic New Orleans Collection, 1971.21i-v.

Perrett, Marvin J. *Nostalgia . . . Lifestyles of "Old" New Orleans.* Published by Marvin J. Perrett, 1982.

Perrett, Marvin J. *More Nostalgia—Legends, Lifestyles, Landmarks.* Published by Marvin J. Perrett, 1982.

Pinistri, S. "New Orleans General Guide & Land Intelligence." New Orleans, 1841, a map housed in The Historic New Orleans Collection, 1960.45i,11.

Popper, Julio. "D. H. Holmes fancy and staple Dry Goods . . . [J. Popper's Map and Directory of the business portion of the city of New Orleans]." New Orleans, 1883, a map housed in The Historic New Orleans Collection, 1955.7i,ii.

Reeves, Sally K. and William D. Reeves. "River Front History," a report commissioned by the Audubon Institute, October 1, 1990.

Robinson, Elisha and R. H. Pidgeon. *Atlas of the City of New Orleans, Louisiana: Based upon Surveys Furnished by John F. Braun.* New York: E. Robinson, 1883.

Schindler, Henri. *Mardi Gras New Orleans.* Paris: Flammarion, 1997.

Tanesse, Jacques. "Plan of the City and Suburbs of New Orleans from an actual Survey made in 1815, New Orleans, 1817. A map housed in The Historic New Orleans Collection, 1971.4.

The Vieux Carré Survey, vols. 1-A, 1-B, 1, 5, 31, 32, 33, 34, 66, 67, 94, and 95, housed at The Historic New Orleans Collection.

Walk, Darlene, coordinator. *Central Business District Neighborhood Profile,* vol. 14A of City of New Orleans Neighborhood Profile Project, New Orleans, 1979.

Walk, Darlene, coordinator. *Mid-City Profile,* vol. 4A of City of New Orleans Neighborhood Profile Project, New Orleans, 1979.

Walk, Darlene, coordinator. *Tulane/Gravier Profile,* vol. 4B of City of New Orleans Neighborhood Profile Project, New Orleans, 1979.

Widmer, Mary Lou. *New Orleans in the Thirties.* Gretna, La.: Pelican, 1989.

Wilson, Samuel, Jr., Patricia Brady, and Lynn Adams, eds. *Queen of the South: New Orleans 1853-1862 the Journal of Thomas K. Wharton.* New Orleans: The Historic New Orleans Collection, 1999.

Wilson, Samuel, Jr. *The Vieux Carré, New Orleans: Its Plan, Its Growth, Its Architeccture,* vol. 7 of "Vieux Carré Historic Demonstration Study," New Orleans, 1968.

Zimpel, Charles F. *Topographical Map of New Orleans and its Vicinity, Embracing a distance of twelve miles up, and eight and three quarter miles down the Mississippi River and Part of Lake Pontchartrain, New Orleans, 1834,* a map housed in The Historic New Orleans Collection, 1955.19a-f.

Index